D1195703

# BORN AGAIN ATHEIST

# BORN AGAIN ATHEIST
## THE ARGUMENTS FOR THE FACTS

*Lance Gregorchuk*

Published 2012 by Enlightened Books

Send enquiries to
Enlightened Books
Im Pfingsterfeld 10
DE 40789 Monheim

www.bornagainatheists.com

Lance Gregorchuk –

Born Again Atheist: The Arguments For The Facts.

Includes references and index.

ILC 4423-573-411-015
1. Religion and Science 2. God-Proof. 3. Atheism

ISBN 978-1-300-23046-5

# Table Of Contents

# *Acknowledgments*

When I undertook the task of writing my first book I did not actually think I would need that much help, as I had been debating those of belief for years and I felt my thoughts were fairly clear; I could not have been more wrong. Without the help of people like John Richards, Chuck Nepps, Alom Shaha, Mathias Kaer, John Brown and Anne Schonhardt I would not have been able to get that precious feedback that one needs to make sure the message and thesis of my book was on course. For your help I am infinitely thankful and indebted to you.

I would also like to thank everyone who participated with me online and in forums on the debate without knowing my actual position. From the religious side: you were extremely helpful making sure that I had a complete understanding of your best arguments. From the atheist side: I did get some excellent ideas from you. Although I have no idea who you are, I want to thank you.

I need to thank my wife who was forced to listen to my arguments into the wee hours of the night when I know she had much better things to do (like sleep), and either shut the arguments down, or more often, calm me in my enthusiasm.

I need to thank my editor Lincoln J. Humphrey, someone who has helped me and forced me to take my thoughts and ideas to the next level. Someone who made me challenge my own thought process and make this book a reality. I have realized these last few months that not unlike Bernie Taupin, Elton John's partner in writing music, the person behind the scene, in this case the editor, actually never gets enough credit for the amazing work that they do from the general public. Finding the right editor for a writer is like finding a soul mate, and LJH was mine.

Finally, I need to thank everyone who told me to write this book and who have encouraged me to do so over the years.

Thank you all for everything you have done in helping make this book a reality.

Lance Gregorchuk

# *Introduction*

A doctrine, whether political or religious, has the same end goal: to get others to believe the central tenets of that doctrine. A leader (or authority figure) must influence an individual to believe what they believe to join their group. The only way, they find, to save their target-group (usually a people, nation, culture or sect) is to indoctrinate them into their system of belief. They invariably start out with just a few convincing ideas, then expand them to comprise whole manifests, e.g. Bibles laid out in hotel rooms by Gideonites, "Lighthouse" booklets handed out by Jehovah's witnesses on street corners or Salafites handing out Korans.

Indoctrination typically begins with the advancement of convincing ideas which are indeed true. For example, all religions embody basic tenets of human interaction, i.e. it's wrong to steal or kill. In fact, in many cases, they were once the first legal codes in their respective cultures. However, they then go further to embody exceptions to those rules, such as it's wrong to kill, *"unless it's an attacking enemy or a threatening enemy,"* or even further, *"unless it's someone who might one day become a threat"* and, in many cases, *"unless it's someone who insults your religion, simply belongs to another religion or merely has no religion."* Ultimately, even killing a person of the same religion – or even killing oneself – is sometimes justified simply because the religious leader orders it. At some point, a line is crossed where the doctrine no longer defines what's morally right but rather allegiance to the group and its leadership.

For group leaders, imbuing a sense of "us against them" is an easier way of assuring group cohesion than championing abstract philosophies of "truth and morality," "convincing ideas" or "platform." The latter is merely used to get people on board. "Fear" and "hope" are prime motivators. Groups employ both. But of the two, "fear of a perceived threat" is what rallies people to action (and garners generous donations ,too).

Sooner or later, "us against them" leads to a conflict with "truth and morality." Would there be no war if everyone was *exclusively* Christian? Would there be no jihads amongst a sea of Islamic practitioners? Would there be no Jewish faith if everyone became a Nazi? And would there be no homosexuals if everyone joined the Southern Baptist Convention?

Protestant vs. Catholic, Hasidic vs. Orthodox, Shia vs. Sunni, communist vs. fascist: whichever one you stake your belief on, there are a dozen more betting, hoping, praying, and opposing – maybe even trying to kill – you simply because they believe you're wrong. At the same time, many of them subscribe to a doctrine espousing freedom of conscience and opinion. What we're left with in each group are factions of varying degrees ranging from fundamentalism (arguably bad) to realism (arguably good).

Slowly but surely, the world is moving away from religion toward secularism. Courts and parliaments, not priests and divine rulers, are now regulating how most people live their lives. However, for better or worse, right now the world is still a cultural and religious melting pot of identities and beliefs. These beliefs still affect the daily lives of everyone and often conflict with one another, whether it be which day of the week is holy (Friday for Muslims, Saturday for Jews, Sunday for Christians), or the societal status of women. Indeed, the fast pace of globalization is bringing the world's religions into closer contact with each other more than ever before. This both heightens the potential for conflict while simultaneously making the virtues of secularism self-evident. In today's world, the role of an atheist is becoming important.

In the face of globalization, both the advance of secularism and the demise of religion appear to be proceeding smoothly. However, among those who do not ascribe to any particular religious mythology, just being atheist and casually observing this process may not be enough. Throughout history, religions have shown enormous staying-power when challenged by adversity. In many cultures, their influence over impressionable groups is widespread. Their education of young children is augmented by various fears (of alien cultures, retribution and invariably of sex), and the care of the sick and elderly is invariably augmented by fears of death.

This book invites its readers to consider whether there is an active role atheists can play – maybe even a moral duty atheists may have. More than just rejecting doctrine, is it indeed an atheist's duty –

in the interest of a peaceful, just and livable world – to differentiate between what is *acceptably* religious and what is *dangerously* religious? This book will help guide the reader's understanding of this concept. It will also give an overview of the scope of the issue and the problems it entails.

What can be found among many of the world's religions is often appalling, frightening, unbelievable, and moreover, *un*godly, as defined by the religions themselves. But that's not all. There are indications doctrinal hegemony – which for millennia had largely been the domain of religions - may now be being usurped by political movements.

In contemporary society, it's becoming increasingly difficult to differentiate religious from political dogma. Both utilize persuasion techniques, group psychology and sometimes coercion to achieve their ends. Typically, their scripture and literature cite historical events which have long ceased to be relevant. The atheist's duty is therefore not a simple task and may sometimes involve careful reexamination of pseudo-historical factoids to challenge the aura of certainty and precision that theology abuses in an effort to cloak itself in civility.

For religions, atheism and secularism have traditionally posed a greater threat than other religions. This may have been because it's easier to get someone to switch Gods than to convince them of the whole concept of a God. For this reason, anyone contemplating active atheism (what this book calls "born again atheism") must be properly prepared. This starts with the knowledge that theologians' favorite argument is to say atheism is just another "belief." In a self-deprecating and sometimes disarming way, they first state they don't "know" there's a God but just "believe" it, adding that they're just like atheists who don't "know" there isn't a God and also just profess to a "belief" that there isn't one. By relegating atheism to "just another dogma," they attempt to create a virtual "level playing field" upon which they can launch their subsequent attacks.

Semantically, atheism has its origins in the Greek language and literally translates as "without God." However, it must be realized, the word "atheism" is used by religious persons to define their opponents. So understandably, it defines them within the frame of reference of a religious person, i.e. in terms of what for them is a given factor - a God, either with or without one. That's not how atheists define themselves. Indeed, among atheists, it's often been suggested a better word is needed. "Secularism" is somewhat better. But it translates more or less as "separationist," implicitly acknowledging a role for religion alongside other institutions of a state. Another term is "humanist," evoking the role of humanity rather than divinity. However, that term has been widely adopted by academia and given a different meaning.

Moving beyond semantics, "atheism" – as defined here – supplants mere "belief" with "thinking, knowing and personal responsibility." It has no "doctrine" like a religion and therefore cannot be compared to one or defined by one. This is essential because religious "doctrines" are the opposite of "thinking." Religions suggest to their followers, *"Don't question or think about it; just believe and do this (i.e., the doctrine)."* The "upside" of such doctrinally ordained behavior can be the avoidance of sinful activity – as defined by the doctrine – which may or may not be actually harmful (i.e. sex before marriage or mass murder). However, the downside is a deactivation of an individual's moral compass. Responsibility for personal actions is delegated to a "God" somewhere out there. Religious people can often be heard to say "it is God's will," "Inschallah," or even "The devil made me do it." Rather than address and modify their own behavior, then will often ask their God for *"forgiveness."* Nothing really changes. Taking this to extremes, rather than asking themselves if it's right or wrong, more impressionable adherants may blow up a bus if they think "non-believers" are on board. This certainly doesn't imply all religious persons are terrorists. It merely illustrates where absolution from personal responsibility by supplanting it with a doctrine can and sometimes does lead.

Atheism is a movement, which is why some have confused it with a religion. However, unlike religions which are organized and have formal political lobbies to secure public funding for self-perpetuating indoctrinational institutions, atheism has so far relied mostly on pure common sense to advance its cause. Although it's done well, in the past that hasn't been enough. Throughout history, competing religious doctrines have played a role in the vast majority of wars. If fanatical religion-like political doctrines are included, almost 100% of all wars are in some way attributable to doctrines having overcome sensible thinking and conscience. So, although it may sound like a cliché, now that opposing sides have nuclear weapons (e.g. Hindu India, Islamic Pakistan, Jewish Israel, Christian USA), the future of humanity now depends on sensible, responsible thinking rather than knee-jerk us-or-them doctrines. What's kept the peace for the past 60 years has been the aptly-named M.A.D. doctrine (Mutually Assured Destruction). What's so absurd about it is that it's the first universally adopted doctrine based entirely on logic. Surely, there's a better way.

The more we willingly accept what should be seen as improbable, impossible, or impractical, the further we regress culturally, scientifically, and intellectually. Indeed, accepting anything without critically examining first is a recipe for disaster. The same applies to atheism itself.

If this book were to take a simplistic *"fundamentalist"* or doctrinational approach to atheism, it would amount to little more than a copy-cat attempt to establish a new religion. Atheism is not just another belief.

Among the many purposes of this book is to address and negate theologians' portrayals of atheism as a "belief," and hopefully dismantling the shroud of *negativism, obstructionism, anti-establishmentism* and even *fanaticism* often associated with non-belief. The goal here is to cause adherants to Muslim, Jewish, Mormon, Christian, Hindu, Buddhist and other faiths not merely to speak out about or against atheism but to truly *contemplate* it as an entirely different philosophy based not on "anti-belief" but on personal responsibility rather than the unseen hand of a God. Yes, the author does occasionally indulge in a few moments of fun taking jabs at the more ludicrous aspects of religious affectations. However, all statements contained herein are made with the intention of provoking actual thought in the best interest of the readership.

Many people assume atheists are simply apathetic to the efforts of religious folk and would rather just not bother with spirituality. This is not the case, but merely an assumption. This author likes the term "anti-theist," championed by the late Christopher Hitchens to distinguish himself from the run-of-the-mill atheist. Essentially, he said, both an atheist and an anti-theist act in accordance with one another. The anti-theist, however, avidly opposes religious ideology, whereas the atheist will only react when provoked and will otherwise generally remain passive, sometimes pointing out how pointless it is to discuss anything with a fundamentalist. An anti-theist looks straight down the barrel of religious hypocrisy, points out the harm it does and questions its existence. "Anti-theists," "active atheists" or "born again atheists" see the danger of religion. They challenge xiv *Born Again Atheist*

religious people to justify their beliefs, sometimes causing them to actually think in the process. A born again atheist will also seek to improve the world by making others aware of the harm religion does.

As an example of such hypocrisy, I once saw an American woman in Dublin, with a small gold cross hanging from her neck, explain to her little girl at the leprechaun museum that "people before used to believe in some very funny things in order to explain the good things and the bad things which were happening, so they blamed it on leprechauns, but they are just stories!" Now, there happens to be an amazing amount of "evidence" supporting their existence; hundreds if not thousands of publications, eye witnesses, and testimonials to the existence of leprechauns. There are even laws in western countries to protect them and give leprechauns *rights*, as well as a voice in the public domain, if they so choose to surface in reality. There is actually a European law protecting leprechauns (and some vegetation) in Ireland, which was written and passed in March of 2011 called the "The Sliabh Foy Loop." In Iceland a similar law exists where if you want to build a house, or clear land, you need to make sure it is approved by elves! These laws are there to protect traditions and folklore, and intended to improve the tourism industries in their respective countries. Even though only very few people take them *literally*, something like this is laughed upon by the same people who believe in all-powerful deities visiting the islands, yet they justify their doctrinal scripture as *right* and *infallible*.

Anytime the anti-theist points out some of the crazy stuff written in Holy Scripture, or various books of different doctrines, then the believer has only a few choices:

1. Take it as face value, strap on a bomb, and deal with the opposition, right up alongside the employees of the abortion clinic, those dancing in a bar in Bali, or those having coffee in Jerusalem.
2. Say: he is God, he can do whatever the hell he likes, and he works in mysterious ways; he giveth and taketh away; he doesn't make mistakes, and it *is* written in *His* book. This person is scarcely discernible form the person described under point "1."
3. The peace-loving clergyman or believer will interpret the law and somehow try to find justification for it.

We step in during situation three, and of course point out the terrors of both one and two. Three, however, is where the problems lie for those particular individuals: they are just stories, evolving from a time where explaining things which people didn't understand was much easier to do by scapegoating with mythologies. People thought volcanoes (and their subsequent eruptions) existed solely on the belief that they erupted on places that were "unholy," and gave reason to why their god destroyed it. The ancient text actually say that nine years, almost to the day, after Roman legionaries destroyed God's house in Jerusalem, God destroyed the luxurious watering holes of the Roman elite, referring to Pompeii and Herculaneum. Obviously there was no other empirical explanation available; therefore, it must have been a god who did it. It took many years afterwards for scientists to develop theories and experiments on plate tectonics, occurring around 1915. This didn't gain much acceptance until the 1960's, and today it is a known fact that the continents drift apart. We can measure it, we can prove it, and after repeated experimentation, we can confirm it as fact. Today we know that volcanoes have nothing to do with a god or gods.

The second primary problem that has to be dealt with is the fact that many of these texts are absolutely *ancient*. Therefore, anyone who now takes part in trying to decode not only their obsolete languages, syntax, and meanings, but also what was originally intended by the text from the beginning is increasingly difficult. Like a sick, demented game of "telephone," naturally these things become misconstrued and contorted over time. Adolf Hitler actually proves this theory quite well. His beliefs and ideology that those belonging to Judaism actually controlled the majority of the economy led his hatred to overtake him; however, this was a mere *interpretation* of the events at hand, and a tremendously rudimentary interpretation at that, negating several factors. Much of this animosity grew from the general discontentedness that most of Europe had as they sought scapegoats for their poor living conditions in the Great Depression. Hitler simply took advantage of this dissatisfaction, and cultivated hatred from its ashes.

What must be understood is that when an individual has a fixated preconception of reality, it is impossible to diminish those deep-rooted intuitions. There is no point in talking with someone who has a bomb strapped to their chest, or trying to explain to that person that their religious leaders have lied to them, that there are no awaiting virgins, and you are not doing the work of your Lord. That person in stage one is too far gone, like Hitler, Polpot, and so many other mentally-wayward people of ideological doctrine before them.

Finally, I wrote this book to help the average layperson stand up against not only the hypocrisy of religions, but their overall exertions, and inevitably, to give the average active atheist the tools they require to counter the arguments a religious person will cite about the existence of God. Yes, I may have also written it to drive them mad; to bring them to a level of frustration where they have to start to question their *own* beliefs, but we have now suffered thousands of years of their religious intolerance, their wars, their genocide, their laws, and their authority as to how we need to grow, adapt, and live in our society.

Why must *we* do this, you ask? The answer: there will always be influential, powerful individuals who abuse a seemingly innocent, morally conducive ideology, just as many have done before. As Clarence Darrow, leading member of the American Civil Liberties Union, once said, "history repeats itself, and that's one of the things that is wrong with history." Let us avoid this redundancy; it is now time to push back this consistent, personal affront on our rights as human beings, and I hope this book helps you do that.

**Lance Gregorchuk**

# CHAPTER 1
## Opening A Debate

*It is said that men may not be the dreams of the Gods, but rather that the Gods are the dreams of men.*

*Carl Sagan*

Since I wrote a book on the practice of debating for the position of the common atheist, I thought I would introduce the content with the original opening transcript of my last debate. I am not quite sure if it was my *best* debate, since normally the public is comprised of 70-80% religious "believers" with the remainder being 10% indifferent and the rest agnostics. I in fact believe that most of the people in the public are *cautious* individuals; we will define *cautious* as those who do not truly believe in the religious fundamentalism of the Bible, but still ritualistically practice baptisms, confirmations, marriages and church worship around Christmas or Easter just to "play it safe."

In a debate, each side gets to open their arguments with an introduction of original content in (approximately) ten minutes. They then move on to the stage of a counter-argument, where they attempt to disprove what has just been promoted. The following excerpt is from a debate I did a few months ago, and I encourage you to utilize whatever pieces work for you in your next religious debate:

I would like to start by saying "thank you" for inviting me today to this debate. I am always excited when I am invited to argue a completely opposing view of anyone who believes, obeys, or worships either the god of Moses, Mohammed, Joseph Smith, Jesus, or even Xenu, the figurehead of Scientology. A debate is where one person holds something to be true, while another holds a different viewpoint; my colleague will attempt to convince you today that his god, which is one of the over hundred gods worshipped today in different countries and cultures around the world, is the right one. Now if you are a person of faith and have ever had the experience of having a Jehovah's Witness or Mormon standing in front of your door, trying to convince you (perhaps someone who believes in the same Abrahamic god as they do) that if you're not doing enough or you're not praying right, you will face the horrors of Hell forever or be denied Heaven on earth, then you will understand the following question: are you not amazed by the conviction with which they say things and the arguments they have?

Those of you who believe in a god may shake your head at their logic; do you not? You laugh because you are correct, as it is not true; it is made up and their final argument, when their faith and all the strange things they believe in are examined by you under a microscope, is finally reduced to"because I just know it" or "look at this text in this scripture here" or "because my parents believe it to be true", simply are not good enough answers for you, are they? My colleague who is debating me tonight may chuckle under his breath or must at least think it a little strange when the Mormon missionary attempts to explain that his brand of "magical underwear," so to speak, is far superior to my colleague's normal underwear, or that you don't go to Heaven but get to be a god on your own planet if you do what his church says; maybe he will consult you about the Jehovah's Witness who believes their sacred books are better translated than your sacred books, and that there is no Heaven and when you die, you go to sleep, only to be woken up by the gentle kiss of God, back in the Garden of Eden?

Yes, my colleague here debating me tonight may probably snort at the Scientologist's beliefs, or even the Rastafarian belief that the leader of Ethiopia Haile Selassie I was really Jesus reincarnate, but what is certain is that my colleague will be firm in his convictions about his god and could definately debate others of different beliefs on their views of their different gods, their different scripture, and explain to them that their different religious symbols, fables and scriptures are completely made up, all the while wholeheartedly embracing the story of the talking snake and donkey, accepting forever the infeasibility of Noah's Ark, even denying the Earth its billions of cherished years of progress and granting it only a few thousand, all the while grasping the cross around his neck because his symbols, his book, and his stories must be true.

My colleague will argue today the case of the "magic man" in the sky, or all around you, perhaps even in the clouds, the all-knowing, all powerful, who could do anything "He" wants, but for some reason chooses to do nothing. How will he attempt to do this? Well, as usual, it will be centrically reliant on *his interpretation* of the word of *his* god; not the god of different people, across vast centuries in different cultures, even on separate continents. Nor will he argue the case for the aboriginal, who bears no importance to the moral codes posed by the Bible, unscathed by the tenets of Western culture. He will also exclude some of your ancestors, who crossed the Bearing Straights during the last Ice Age to North America 4,000 to 6,000 years before his god was ever dreamed up. He must ascribe his beliefs to what he and others have interpreted in the translation of a book.

Will he deny that people walked over the Bearing Straights; will he deny Neanderthal Man who lived, flourished, before his god created the earth? Well I certainly, for all sake of his logic, assume so; yet whatever his argument, his justifications, and his support of those justifications for the *facts* of the existence of his god, must directly come from scripture: what was written in and translated from his book. My colleague will use scripture in many of the arguments he has, and this will, for him, be absolute proof, because how could his book of fairy tales, his god's book of magic, be wrong? Yet, I have read the Bible, The Qur'an, The Book of Mormon and Mein Kämpf and can also quote his holy book and many others as well, but watch when I use the exact same scripture, the exact same words by the exact same author of the exact same book to prove my point.

What is written in his book is not real, is made up, is not full of peace and love and the answers to all things in the universe, but rather hate, persecution, threats, and fables. Yes, he will dismiss my argument as pertaining to a "lack of understanding," a misinterpretation; that I failed to truly interpret it the way the Lord intended it to be interpreted; that I fail to understand that when an individual writes one thing, his true intent is  something entirely different.

Maybe this makes me ignorant, as when I hear a person say something, I generally imagine that they *mean* it. But maybe, as he puts it, I don't have the "gift of faith." I will tell you now, I do not want the burden, just as much as I don't want to believe, I *cannot* believe, in a talking snake, Jonah living in a whale, the ridiculousness of Noah's Ark, or the Earth being a mere 6,000 years old; nor can I buy into a space god named Xenu, or the Judaic philosophy that I can't eat pork sausages; neither will I accept that I must pray five times a day in the direction of Mecca, and that if I blow myself up for "the cause" there will be 72 virgins waiting for me, or that if a young woman is raped by her uncle and gets pregnant, she should be denied an abortion, because that is what his god "wants."

Watch my colleague as he discusses issues and he uses Leviticus, Deuteronomy, or Judges to prove a point, or when he uses Matthew and Mark to reinforce his argument. Yet when I do the exact same thing, when I use those same people, when I show you and him what they said at a different time in the book, we will watch as, like clockwork, it turns out that it must be me who is misinterpreting the text he interprets so well, so sometimes his scripture will mean what it says, and other times we will *need his interpretation* of the meaning, according to him.

Once we have proven that his book of fairy tales is fictional, that the stories are not true, and that the earth was not created by his god, my colleague may then attempt to utilize science in his argument; he may even bring up the Second Law of Thermodynamics, or intelligent design theory; perhaps he will try to deny macroevolution, all the while supporting microevolution. No, he will not deny that there were no dogs in Noah's Ark as he knows dogs actually evolved from wolves, and that all dogs today, the big ones and small ones, the ones with hair and the ones without, the vast amazing differences in all canine types today all evolved from wolves, although this "dogs evolving from wolves" is still a theory 99.99% of all scientists, biologists, anthropologists, and even Christian (dare I say the word "Scientists") agree with, and so will he; yet in the same breath he will deny that there is any way we humans could have evolved from apes as he *must* say this, or his book is completely wrong. Imagine that, although we can watch evolution unfold before our very eyes, he will deny, he *must* deny, that we evolved. In order to believe in God, truly, you must deny evidence and facts, which he will say he doesn't but which I will prove he has.

At last, he will bring out the final "trump" card: maybe God *instigated* the Big Bang, instilling the universe with light and life, impossibly and infinitesimally editing with the finesse of a watchmaker (because how else could this have all appeared here if not from some sort of "god in the missing parts" that science hasn't yet proven with certitude as of yet). One thing is for certain, however: if he does argue that, this will prove that his book of stories which he holds as dear as the truth is simply null and void.

One thing must be noted. You may not choose one segment of the Bible and ignore the rest. This, unfortunately for the believers out there, will be the resulting findings of today's debate. Either the Bible is correct and there are indeed talking snakes, the world *was* created in 6,000 years, and Noah just forgot about the fish and kangaroos, and God sent his only son, birthed of a virgin mother in Bethlehem on Christmas day, to die on the cross. Or, as I will illuminate, perhaps we simply attribute our understanding of the universe to fact, science, and inscrutable evidence. When it is convenient, he will say that the Bible is 100% true, and when not, he will say that he and a handful of others can successfully interpret the words of scripture where you and I could not. I am sure had this debate been taking place 300 years ago, I would be the heretic arguing the Heliocentric Theory of Copernicus, and he would be reading scripture pleading that the flat earth is the center of the universe and the sun revolves around us.

Please take note, and I say this upfront, as you watch my colleague dance around the subject of evidence and facts when I question him on the above mentioned mythologies, by which he will attempt to say that on one hand we have fables and life lessons and the other literal truths; he will deny the validity of some stories and dismiss them as cultural and timely irrelevant, all the while utilizing others for his fundamentalist arguments. This applies to any and all scenarios, whether we are discussing the religious arguments related to homosexuality, marriage, morality, women's issues, contraception, Heaven and Hell, and the fact that his god went from showing himself through the parting of the Red Sea to surprising a child at breakfast on a slice of burnt toast (which is now a viral YouTube video with 2.7 million views, I may add), and that *this* must be today the evidence, the miracle, confirming that his god is real.

His god does not exist, but to admit this would be contrary to his profession: he sells to other people everything in the next life, all the while enjoying the royalties he and his corresponding church enjoy in the present one. Religion is for the weak, the sick, the dying, and the insecure, young and impressionable individuals on the earth exploited by men searching for power or justifications for their actions. It is for the poor, and the unreasonable, and my colleague is firmly aware of this; his book, along with his interpretations, will promise you everything in the next life as long as you do everything he asks in this life.

Yes, I do see his religion as what it is: it does take *faith* to believe that a god could order the genocide of an entire people, or direct and condone the rape of innocent young women. His god can easily condemn children, whose only crime they ever committed was to not pray to the Abrahamic god, and when questioned about it, like Donald Rumsfeld after realizing the absence of weapons of mass destruction, will turn a blind eye and say: "We are beyond that now." Like Rumsfeld, only a few ever interpreted his God's actions as that of a war criminal, yet you know it and I know it, if you put his God on trial in the Haag, he would rot in a cell for eternity for his crimes against humanity. Yet isn't it ironic, funny even, that if his god received eternity in prison from the international court for what he did, we would not kill him, we would not put him to death, because we as humans are above that. Unfortunately for him, his god isn't real, or he would be on trial. The religious leaders of today know that, like Machiavelli said, "[m]en are so simple of mind, and so dominated by their immediate needs, that a deceitful man will always find plenty who are ready to be deceived."

My colleague will continue to find so many ways to deceive you, even as honest as his intentions may seem to be, religion and religious leaders have but just one goal: money and subsequent power. If they were serious, for instance, about eradicating poverty significantly, they would sell their expansive assets and distribute them, investing in clean drinking sources for people in third world countries, maybe helping them purchase and set up farming for livestock, and provide support to the impoverished and oppressed women, who fundamentally, as we all know, are the backbone of a society and the individuals who can fix a society from the inside out. If his church were so serious about "helping" others, shouldn't they donate all or most of their wealth? I am not talking about *some* of his church's wealth; I am talking about the feasible majority of it: sell everything. If you think your god is judging you for what you do in this life, then go and be just like Mother Theresa, who forever provided charity to those in need, and who herself was more of a Christ-like figure than Jesus himself.

Speaking of Mother Theresa, religious individuals attempt to cover up her disdain for religion. The evidence is found in her diaries and memoirs written towards the end of her life, and in them, she discloses her personal information. Just as his Jesus once asked "why hath thou forsaken me?" Mother Theresa wrote[1]:

Lord, my God, you have thrown [me] away as unwanted – unloved. I call, I cling, I want, and there is no one to answer, no, no one. Alone. Where is my faith? Even deep down there is nothing. I have no faith. I dare not utter the words and thoughts that crowd in my heart... Did I make a mistake in surrendering blindly to the Call of the Sacred Heart?

She even compared her problems to Hell, admitting that she had begun to doubt the existence of Heaven and God. But even the church would not allow that to stop them from making her a saint. Why, you may ask? They attributed her doubt to a test from God himself; all the while watching with complete indifference the pain, suffering, and dying of millions of innocent children.

Certainly, her bosses could have sold some of their art work, maybe a property or two to truly help Mother Theresa in her cause, but instead, they sold Mother Theresa the ultimate price, didn't they? Just like the suicide bomber who questions his faith seconds before he blows himself up, Mother Theresa knew at the end that there was no God. Now ask yourself this: "if your god wouldn't do anything for her, if he wouldn't help her, why would he do anything for you?" This is his plan? This is completely opposite of the assumptions we have made about God by this juncture.

And this is what my colleague is going to try to argue tonight. We will talk about his god, all of his views on sexuality, women, the morality of religion and about his book and the fables within, and much more tonight. But remember this: if all that is left at the end of the night is "because I have faith," then he could have been just as easily arguing the case for magic underwear, leprechauns or unicorns. I will not just show you tonight how hypocritical his faith is; I will not only point out the blatantly obvious and back it up with scientific data, but I will show you today that just as there are no leprechauns, nor a pot of gold at the end of a rainbow, there is no god or gods among us.

---

[1] Published letters of Mother Theresa

# CHAPTER 2
## *The Ten Commandments*

*And behold, one came up to him, saying, "Teacher, what good deed must I do, to have eternal life?"*

*And he (Jesus) said to him, "Why do you ask me about what is good? One there is who is good. If you would enter life, keep the commandments."*

Matthew 19:16-17

Many Christians believe that without the Bible they would not be able to understand the world or the differences between right and wrong, they would cheat on their wives daily, kill their neighbors for smiting them and go to the bank only to rob it at gun point. The belief that the Ten Commandments are the foundation to their religion, and that it guides them, is something I have always found a bit perplexing, as I have never been one to just sit back and accept words. I have always looked into their meaning. Personally, I cannot imagine repeating text over and over again in a mosque, or at the Wailing Wall rocking from forward to back, for the sake of memorizing text without ever wanting to understand what the words that I was repeating actually *meant*. As a young catholic, you are asked to repeat the Lord's Prayer over and over again, the apostle's creed and the Hail Mary. These are often given out as punishment after confessing your sins; like eight Hail Marys and six Lord's Prayers would really get a 12 year old out of hell for intentionally tripping Billy Elson at a soccer game.

Yet as the punishment was revealed to me I actually, even as a 12 year old, didn't just say the words on autopilot; as a young person I wanted to understand their significance, and when I did research the results were troubling. There are some glaring and significant problems with the foundational guide of Christian philosophy, and subsequently, their morality, referred to as the "Ten Commandments." In some school districts around the world, schools and teachers are pressured to teach the Ten Commandments alongside general biology in the classroom. It is definitely an advantage for atheists and children who do not want to believe in the fairy tales worshipped by Christians to further understand what exactly they believe, and fundamentally, what exactly the Ten Commandments are intending to profess.

Once again, most Christians have a very rudimentary idea of what they are talking about when they are referencing the Ten Commandments; there were many times in the past where I would ask a Christian what his or her favorite commandment was, and which one would provide me with the best "moral compass." Is "Thou shalt not rape women" his favorite? Or maybe his favorite is "Thou shalt not commit genocide?" Unfortunately, those two are not there. The commandments teach *Christians* how to live moral and ethical lives, really asserting their edge over and above atheists and "inferior" religions. But as soon as we begin to scrutinize the foundations of the Ten Commandments and those who ascribe to them, what then is left?

First, we know that these were commandments and that there were ten of them, and just about everyone knows the story behind them; however, different religions have had issues with them. These commandments are located in two sections of the Bible: Exodus 20:1-17 and Deuteronomy 5:4-21. Although Catholics focus upon Deuteronomy, there are many Protestants who use the Exodus version, alongside their religious cousins the Lutherans. However, if you begin to ask a Christian to name all ten, they usually only get to a maximum of six at best; most really just get to four. If you put down this book right now and conjure up all ten Commandments off-the-cuff, I would be tremendously surprised, as they are strange focal points for a philosophy if you take them literally, or begin to try to plainly interpret what they are intending to say.

Let's begin by asking you this: when you are putting together a list of anything you want or desire, don't the important ones get written down first? Aren't they written sequentially in the list, ranging from most to least in terms of importance? If you had to make a list of the ten things you wanted your kids to accomplish in life, I am guessing the most vital things would come first. With this logic in place, how about we begin a shopping list. When we begin take a moment to stop and analyze each and every one of the commandments, you will notice the placement of each is dripping with what a culture hundreds of years before valued and cherished.

*1) Thou shalt have no other gods before me.*

Essentially, this means that unlike Muslims, who are monotheistic (believe in one god), Christians can have as many gods as they please, as long as they do not come before the important, central God; similar to this is the Greeks' Zeus, who has a pantheon of other gods before him. If you look at the actual law, you will see that the Christian god recognizes the "existence," and/or possibility of the existence, of other gods. This is the reason Christians allow the entry of the Holy Spirit and Jesus Christ, while Catholics allow the saints or the Pope, who they view as infallible; they also believe that "he" (it can only be a man) is the vicar of Christ, the earthly representative of God or Christ. But, you can have other gods as a Christian, which is important to remember as Christians ascribe to the theory of monotheism, which illuminates the obvious: this commandment essentially allows the worship of a golden cow, or even a space monkey, as long as you put the Big Guy upfront (remember, the commandment states *Thou shalt have no other gods before me;* it says nothing about *after)*. Compare this to the Qur'an, which is very clear that there is only one God; Allah. "There is no god but Allah" is the basic attitude of Islam. There is no ambiguity about this in the Qur'an and there are hundreds of verses in the Qur'an that make this point very clear.

**2) Thou shalt not make thee any graven image or any likeness of any thing that is in heaven above, or that is on the earth beneath, or that is in the waters beneath the earth.**

This is the commandment which Christians regularly fail to remember, and incongruously so, being that it seems to be number two on their list of important things. Truthfully, Christians should actually *hate* this commandment; those pictures of Jesus Christ or God, of the Holy Gates, Saint Peter, or Hell – all the wonderful illustrations laden in children's Bibles and stories: these pictures represent and equate to condemnation in Hell. Remember, this is a *commandment!* It is just as important as murder, or adultery, as it was included amongst them. This commandment will essentially direct a Christian (especially a Catholic) to commit a sin every instant they are in their place of worship. Just possessing and fondling a rosary or cross could be interpreted, fundamentally, as a slide against God. Worse yet, even pictures of *bread*\* could reasonably fall into this category. Do not draw *bread?* Let's begin to elaborate upon this from a purely logical standpoint.

> If we must take the Bible from a literal, fundamentalist standpoint, during the Last Supper, Jesus Christ's body was represented in the form of bread.
>
> Recall that Jesus Christ, in Christian theology, represents one-third of God, this being "God the Son."
>
> He gave this bread to his disciples, and proclaimed "Take, eat; this is my body."
>
> If logic prevails, we can assume that, as the body of Christ, bread can fall amongst the category of *"anything"* from the second commandment, this being on "earth beneath," which is in *likeness* of God.
>
> Therefore, an illustration of bread should be a slight against the Christian god, being that they "practice what they preach," so to speak.

Furthermore, there should be no pictures or representations of God! None, which includes   Michelangelo's *Sistine Chapel* and Leonardo Da Vinci's famous *Last Supper*, two of the most obvious examples amidst a sea of theological artwork. And what about *"Thou shalt not make thee any graven image ....***or that is in the waters beneath the earth.***"* So, in other words, do not draw fish! Drawing fish is a bad thing. But have you ever seen how born-again Christians have that bumper sticker with that picture of the fish on their cars so you can recognize them as born-agains? Guess what: they are going to Hell, as technically that is a picture of something that is in the waters beneath the earth.

Beginning on March 2, 2001, a group of radical Muslims known as the Taliban began their campaign to destroy two revered Buddhist statues in the Bamyan province in Afghanistan. The attack was dictated by Taliban leader Mullah Mohammed Omar, and represented their religious fundamentalism against "idolatry." If you were to ask a Christian why this is unacceptable, whilst their own commandment advocates or implies the identical message, they will be hard-pressed to respond; they will even go to great lengths to distance themselves from Islamic religion, even given their ancestral nature.

Here is the second and more severe problem with the second most important thing to a Christian. Read the commandment again:

Thou shalt not make thee *any* graven image, *or* any likeness *of anything* that is in heaven above, or that is on the earth beneath, or that is in the waters beneath the earth.

You cannot even speak about it! A preacher telling his flock about Heaven and how great it is "up there," or how unfortunate and horrific it is "down below" is making an image; is painting a portrait; is making a likeness thereof. What preacher or religious leader is granted the allowance to do so, we ask? There is, according to Christian law, none to be noted or accounted for. Of course, you will read arguments from Christians that this is not what was intended by the commandment when it was given to Moses, but then that presents a paradox; the sentence was written in such a way as to there being no possibility of misinterpretation. It was written as concisely and directly as a vibrant "Stop" sign on the side of the road.

### 3) *Thou shalt not take the name of the Lord thy God in vain: for the Lord will not hold him guiltless that taketh his name in vain.*

Seriously? This is number three of the list of important things to remember, to be considerate of? I am just wondering how many individuals at the time were proclaiming "Golden Ram you are correct!" or "God of the Maneates be Damned!" in exasperation for this to maintain importance. Essentially, this commandment could be used to morally reprimand the usage of a number of common phrases uttered by contemporary society, such as the ever over-used "Thank God," or "Goodbye" (which originated from the Old English phrase "God Be With You"). Or if you attempt to align previous morale, it could be that utilizing "Jesus H. Christ" in a sentence is fine, because according to the first commandment, it doesn't refer to the *main* Christian god; of course, consistency has never been a Christian's strong-suit.

Nevertheless, this was fundamental for God's shopping list, and, as with all of the other commandments, cannot be simply overlooked, as those who worship have a tendency to do. It is important to note that, amongst the list of commandments, this commandment is typically common knowledge when conjured up on a whim by the casual, strolling Christian. Is this, perhaps, indicative of the dire importance of the third commandment?

### 4) *Keep the Sabbath day to sanctify it, as the Lord thy God hath commanded thee.*

It is at this point in the Ten Commandments where things become thorny, however there is no rose at the end of the stem. Originally, the Sabbath being referred to was practiced on Saturday. This was, at the time, considered to be Mosaic Law, or the Law of Moses. The conflict arises when we realize that Mosaic Law is only applicable to those who abide by it: the Jews. It is interesting to analyze the Christian belief that the Ten Commandments were and are entirely applicable to their lives, when at least one of these commandments never intended to include them. So what reasoning does the average Christian give for this logical conundrum? One must look at the history to find the true answers.

The only interval during which Christianity was unified about celebrating on Saturday or Sunday occurred between the crucifixion of Jesus Christ, circa 30 CE, and the arrival of Paul the Apostle in Judea near the end of that decade. The Jewish-Christian movement was under the leadership of James – the Apostle of Jesus, and brother of John the Apostle. They sacrificed in the Temple and observed the Laws of Moses; that is, until the late 4th century CE, when Christianity was made the official religion of Rome. At the point previous, Christians lived in a predominately Pagan society. This was the long-established, official religion of the Roman Empire, which consisted of a mosaic of Pagan varietals. It involved a worship of – and nominal sacrifice to – a pantheon of Roman deities, both gods and goddesses.

A strong competitor to Christianity in those days, next to Paganism, was a religion called Mithraism. This faith was practiced by the people of Persia, and their surrounding provinces. It became popular amongst Roman civil serviceman and military. Even those in Mithraic religion practiced a form of the Sabbatical, and worshipped gods and goddesses similar to those of Pagan culture in the northwest. There were many smaller religions aside from these two that initially composed the greater Eastern world, all sharing common principles and, fundamentally, religious practices. Many Christians were tempted to follow suit.

Although the Christians were motivated to follow alongside the Pagans and Jewish faiths, they were also motivated to change the day of Sabbath as a method of distancing themselves from them. There are two primary reasons behind this:

1) The Roman government had begun a campaign against the Jewish faith, intermittently persecuting them; it was safer for Christianity to be considered a separate entity.
2) Relations between the Jews and Christians were hostile at this time. The early Christian church suffered much persecution from the Jews.

In 321 CE, while he was a Pagan worshipper, the Emperor Constantine declared that *Sunday* was going to be the day of rest throughout the Roman Empire:

On the venerable day of the Sun let the magistrates and people residing in cities rest, and let all workshops be closed. In the country however persons engaged in agriculture may freely and lawfully continue their pursuits because it often happens that another day is not suitable for grain-sowing or vine planting; lest by neglecting the proper moment for such operations the bounty of Heaven should be lost[2]."

The Church Council of Laodicea, circa 364 CE, ordered that the religious observances of Christian faith were to be observed on a Sunday, rather than the Jewish Saturday. They ruled that "Christians shall not Judaize and be idle on Saturday, but shall work on that day."[3] Many indicators in history suggest that Christians initially *ignored* the proclamation. In as late as 1115 CE, Sabbath observance was noted in Wales. In 1560 CE, Francis Xavier, co-founder of the

---

[2] MacMullen 1969; *New Catholic Encyclopedia*, 1908; *Theodosian Code*.
[3] A History of the Councils of the Church, Vol. 2, p. 316

"Society of Jesus" (a Catholic male religious order), was concerned about Sabbath worship in Goa, India; his solution: an Inquisition in order to establish ground and eradicate "Jewish wickedness" from the surrounding area. A Catholic provincial council entirely suppressed the practice in Norway around 1435 CE[4].

If those of the Jewish faith assert that the original message of God was to practice upon Saturday, while the Christians and their leaders essentially attempt to alter that original commandment, what importance should we who attempt to analyze it realistically ascribe to it? Are they just mere words? The importance of noting the amount of conflict, debate, and confusion amongst the religious fundamentalists on this commandment appertains to this fact: if one aspect of any of the Bible is logically fallacious, that means that part or all of the remainder is fallacious as well.

### 5) Honour thy father and thy mother, as the Lord thy God hath commanded thee; that thy days may be prolonged, and that it may go well with thee, in the land which the Lord thy God giveth thee.

This is actually a commandment that a good majority of contemporary society, naturally, can and will generally subscribe to; yet, Jesus wasn't its greatest advocate:

If any man come to me, and hate not his father, and hate not his mother... he cannot be my disciple (Luke 14:26).

Nevertheless, one significant and intriguing aspect of this commandment is that, during the time in which human beings wrote it, women weren't given any credence in relation to men; in this commandment, they are treated as equals. This stands in direct contrast to sections amongst the Bible, in which women were given subordinate status, such as in Deuteronomy:

When men strive together one with another, and the wife of the one draweth near for to deliver her husband out of the hand of him that smiteth him, and putteth forth her hand, and taketh him by the secrets (25:11):

Then thou shalt cut off her hand, thine eye shall not pity her (25:12).

---

[4] Church Council held at Bergin, August 22,1435

In contemporary society, this amount of male chauvinism is enough to result in social exile; in the times of the Old Testament, it was perfectly reasonable. It does appear off that when God gave his commandments to Moses, his original intent was explicitly related to the notion of *equality*, whereas historically, Christians and their contemporaries treated women like their common farm animals. You would think that if God had meant something different, he may have added a cliff note. Christians would argue that this is irrelevant, and that mankind made the errors, rather than their god; then perhaps these individuals weren't particularly dedicated to begin with.

As a clarifying point, it is very important than we focus on the last segment of the commandment:

…that thy days may be prolonged, and that it may go well with thee, *in the land which the Lord thy God giveth thee.*

One could argue that what God originally intended was that he meant only to "[h]onour" your mother and father within the land of Israel, or it could have been the original surrounding land of Moses' geographical birth place of Egypt. If the Christians and Jews in the times of the Old Testament can contradict the commandment of God, then a skeptic can begin to question the specifics of the commandment and its implications.

This commandment is one of the few commandments that have become socially irrelevant however true-to-the-heart the principle presumes itself to be. Social familial structure has changed over the course of the centuries since the commandments were scripted, and the male has become less important for the female and child's survival. Therefore, we must question whether this commandment bears any importance any longer.

For instance, what if we were to pose that a child who grew up within an orthodox Christian religion was abused emotionally, physically, and sexually, *repeatedly* throughout his or her development. Other than the permanent damage instilled upon it, would the members of his or her related church brush the implications off because their god had commanded them to honor the father or mother who had abused said child? We in contemporary society would think not; but it is a *commandment*, one that must be followed because it is the *law of God* himself. If one fails to follow one of God's most important rules, then they must acknowledge that they themselves have failed God. These are the instances where fairness and forgiveness are all but a double-standard to fundamentalists.

## 6) *Thou shalt not kill.*

Many people have simply come to terms with this commandment, as it is pretty straight forward and gives no room for leniency. Most of us, religious or non-religious, have constructed our moral precipice at the boundary of killing another human being. But how far should the rational individual take this commandment? Should we all live vegan or vegetarian lifestyles in the name of God, just because those of us who don't would be *killing* and eating animals?

Social and political boundaries aside, there are some serious contradictions by God himself in the Old Testament, as accounted for in the book of Joshua:

And the Lord said unto Joshua, 'Be not afraid because of them: for tomorrow about this time will I deliver them up all slain before Israel: thou shalt hough their horses, and burn their chariots with fire (11:6).

And according to the passages in all translations and editions of the Bible, that is precisely what God proceeded to do. After killing a few hundred people, this is the passage provided:

And they smote all the souls that were therein with the edge of the sword, utterly destroying them: there was not any left to breathe: and he burnt Hazor with fire. (Joshua 11:11)

This is in reference to the occupation of the city of Hazor (located in Canaan; modern Israel) by a tribe of individuals governed by King Jabin. This area was considered the Promised Land, and the Jews the Promised Land's people; God did not appreciate Jabin and his people in the Promised Land. So God gave this order to Moses, who gave the order to Joshua. As logic plays out, and logic is all we have to give, God gave the order to Joshua; in a modern context, that means that God is the principal in the murder of hundreds of individuals; the Charles Manson of religious text. And if this is true, as is proposed, then why didn't Jesus simply denounce his own father? Could this be because his father commanded him to "[h]onour thy father"?

The common Christian argument is this: God is God, and you are not. If he can create life, as proposed by Christian mythology, then he just as assuredly can take life as he sees fit. It is funny to note though that according to the Bible, God kills over 2 million people[5] and this is excepting the victims of Noah`s flood, Sodom and Gomorrah, or the many plagues, famines, fiery serpents, etc. because no specific numbers were given[6]. If we take this at face-value, then we can just as easily come to the conclusion that the creator of our universe doesn't follow one of his ten universal principles; I am almost certain that a presidential leader would (as they often do) have issues with re-election amongst the electorate public if that individual slid against their own principles. God is given a pass in Christian mythos.

It is a common assumption that God had given Israel a "civil authority" over the rest of the surrounding land, which is the explanation by the Christian authorities given for the above described genocide of the Canaanites. In a modern context, this could be analogized to a high court ordering the death of an inmate in order to replace that inmate with another; one person (or people, in this case) are given preference by God over another, and in God's eyes, the murder of another person or group of people is justified if, essentially, it is for the betterment of another group of people. Thou shalt not kill, unless, of course, you really want what another individual has.

## 7) *Thou shalt not commit adultery.*

In contemporary Western society, just as with the previous commandment, most are in agreeance. For a quick definition of adultery, Webster has given us this:

voluntary sexual intercourse between a married man and someone other than his wife, or between a married woman and someone other than her husband.

---

[5] Gen 41:25-54, Ex 9:25, Ex 12:29-30, Num 16:49, Num 25:1-11, Num 31:1-35, Dt 3:3-6, Jos 8:1-25, Heb 11.32, 1Sam 2:25 and many more examples including his own son.

[6] And since it is a debate we need to also say that the Devil is responsible for killing 10 people: The seven sons and three daughters of Job. *And he only does this because god allowed it as part of a running bet he made with him during a conversation where* God tells Satan to do nasty things to Job to see if he can get Job to curse God to his face. Technically the blood is on god's hands for these as well. Job 1-1:22

Now, keep in mind that this is the fashionable, modern version of this definition. In Biblical times, things were slightly different. When God gave Moses the order to continue his genocidal campaign, now against all the kings of Midian, he had no qualms about who was meant to live, or who was meant to remain "unadulterated," so to speak. To exemplify this point, regard the following passages from Numbers:

Moses, Eleazar the priest and all the leaders of the community went to meet them outside the camp (31:13). Moses was angry with the officers of the army —the commanders of thousands and commanders of hundreds—who returned from the battle (31:14).

Have you allowed all the women to live?' he asked them (31:15). 'They were the ones who followed Balaam's advice and enticed the Israelites to be unfaithful to the Lord in the Peor incident, so that a plague struck the Lord's people (3:16). Now kill all the boys. And kill every woman who has slept with a man, but save for yourselves every girl who has never slept with a man (31:17).

According to these passages, these young girls, which modern citizens would consider victims of sexual abuse (and the men morally bankrupt), are simply "plunder" for the soldiers; synonymous to cattle or money. In modern law, we refer to this practice as "statutory rape," pertaining to anyone under the age of legal consent. Now, granted, the times in which this occurred were vastly different from today's legal structure. Therefore, it may be unfair to judge individuals who committed these acts solely on this principle. However, the emphasis must be applied to the notion that these soldiers, the majority assumedly married, were committing or had the intent to commit sex acts with unwilling girls; this was commanded by Moses, prophet and messenger of God. This latter emphasis is to counter the Christian argument that this was man's folly, rather than something God intended. This is simply, as proven above, erroneous.

## 8) *Thou shall not steal.*

If we look back upon God's orders to take back the Promised Land from the Canaanite occupants, or for that matter the Midianites, one could interpret these acts as "stealing," to explain it rudimentarily. Of course, as with murder, it is justified since those who are committing the act are worthy of its plunders. Even those who attacked and murdered the Midianites were committing theft, as this passage from Numbers suggests:

And the children of Israel took all the women of Midian captives, and their little ones, and took the spoil of all their cattle, and all their flocks, and all their goods. And they burnt all their cities wherein they dwelt, and all their goodly castles, with fire. And they took all the spoil, and all the prey, both of men and of beasts (31:9-11).

We are going to assume when they refer to "children of Israel," that the author is referring to the general population of Israel, or the Bible may indeed be as twisted as some presume. Now, at this point, that means every individual involved in the massacre committed theft of property that, although owned by the recently deceased, was blatantly not originally the Israelite's property. Therein proposes just another contradiction: this was all done on God's command. He indeed was the mastermind in this most disturbing of plots; he commanded the murdering and plundering of the people of Midian amongst thousands of others. So how could God possibly reconcile the theft and murder of these seemingly innocent people? The answer is self-explanatory.

## 9) *Thou shalt not bear false witness against thy neighbor.*

This commandment is another which falls into the genres of *What?* and *Why?*, especially when positioned cozily next to the last three commandments. This is another commandment which begs to be overanalyzed, simply because it gives the reader so little. Let's begin by defining "false witness," as that is a rather vague phrase. Original Christian scholars attribute this phrase directly to the concept of lying in the commission of providing testimony in trial. But if that were to be the case, does that mean that the court is "thy neighbor"? This may present itself to be an ignorant question, but it is begging the rest of the question: if it is simply the court, then that means you can bear false witness to your literal neighbor with no reprimand by God. Of course, modern Christians argue that this commandment essentially bars *all* forms of lying, rather than just legal testimonials.

And this introduces another question, albeit a more personal one. Why must fundamentalists insist on creating an over-arching umbrella of morality, especially when you consider this amendment to be one miniscule rain drop in a massive moral ocean? Its literal, historical definition is simple: Do not lie in court. Of course, we can also assume, like so many other associated problems, the original text was misconstrued from the beginning, and that modern Christians are correct. Given this, let's play around with a scenario.

*It is the birthday of your neighbor (assuming you actually appreciate your neighbor). You and your family have decided that you would like to throw him a surprise party. There are several occasions when your neighbor has a sneaking suspicion that your family is up to something. On one of these occasions, your neighbor directly asks you whether or not you are trying to throw a surprise party in his honor. You tell him directly no, and that you have no idea what he is talking about; you may even imply he is "losing it," for the purpose of conviction. The next day is his birthday, and you invite him over for dinner. Your family surprises him with balloons, a barbeque, cake, and a pat on the back.*

In this scenario, you have just sinned against God; once again, assuming that you believe in that sort of mythology. You have literally taken it upon yourself to "bear false witness to [your] neighbor," given that we use the broad definition given by the modern Christian. Does this really warrant the kind of Hell consistently painted that you may or may not end up in? Will God consider this to be the ultimate end-all scenario against him? As a skeptic, these are the questions in which we must invest ourselves, however seemingly ludicrous they may present themselves to be.

## 10) *Thou shalt not covet thy neighbour's wife, nor his manservant, nor his maidservant, nor his ox, nor his ass, nor any thing that is thy neighbour's.*

It remains to this day perplexing to assume that this would even be on the list; you would think God would simply add this as a footnote, or amendment to his moral Constitution, than add it in full to his collection. George Orwell inadvertently provided a perfect analogy to this commandment when he wrote his monumental *1984*. In this novel, there exists the "Thought Police," whose sole purpose is to uncover and punish "thought crimes." Essentially, God is acting as the Thought Police, wherein he punishes those whose mind wanders from the reasonable ("Perhaps I may sleep with my neighbor's wife today") to the trivial ("I really would enjoy driving my neighbor's Miata"). These small subconscious entries could land a much-feared seat in the fire depths, and there is no reasonable justification for it. We can even go as far as to define, much as they did in Biblical times, "thy neighbor" as the court; in which case, coveting anything of the court's is simply *silly*, as there can only be so many uses for a mallet.

Could it be, perhaps, that the reason for this confusion about what precisely each of these commandments intends stems from mental constructs of no omniscient deity, but individuals of different moral fiber, cultures, and faiths? You would assume that if God was powerful enough to create man, who is forever progressing through limitless consciousness and scientific exploration, he could at least perfect a list of ten separate ideas. Perhaps we should mandate a revising or reinterpretation of these commandments to bring them up to par with modern society's norms and values, and correct the folly and mistakes made by mankind hundreds of years before.

I once conversed with my seven year old boy, whose school was teaching him about the Ten Commandments (a situation I have had much contention with, and will be described in full in the proceeding chapters), that if he had the wherewithal to write the Ten Commandments over, which list he would choose. The following is precisely what he wrote down (with reasonable spelling corrections):

1)  Don't kill other people.

2)  Be nice to other people.

3)  Don't hurt animals.

4)  Wear your seatbelt.

5)  Say please and thank you.

6)  Play fair.

7)  Don't call people names.

8)  There should be no war.

9)  Don't pollute.

10) Separate your garbage.

I believe his list is a big improvement on the Christians'. Don't you?

# CHAPTER 3

## *Hell*

*The trouble with theocracy is that everyone wants to be Theo.*

*James Dunn*

In 1979, my family had finally invested in a color television, and I found it tremendously fascinating. I loved Saturday mornings, as you could watch an array of imaginative, and at that age, enlightening cartoons. Among these, you had the infamous He-Man, The Smurfs, or Rainbow Brite. As a child, we were only allotted two days a week to have fun; to play; to be children. One of these days became dedicated to church service, and you can already assume which one it was. As a Catholic, that entire day's course was altered. We had the actual church service for an hour; after that, catechism for another hour. Post-catechism usually involved speaking to parents about the two hours prior, which typically ended in yet another hour. We went to church on Sundays at noon; this is vivid, because I know precisely how much it stunted the fun and progress of the day. So from noon to approximately 4 PM, my life was centrically, coercively, religious. By the end of it all, it was supper time, which predicated bedtime. I wanted my Sunday for me, not for a god that never responded to my demands; not for a god that took my scarce time for personal recreation away either.

I noticed that just down the street, however, children were going to church at 9 AM. This meant that they could get church out of the way earlier, and I grew incredibly jealous of that fact. My parents explained to me that they were Pentecostal, which for a child is gibberish, in much the same way their child probably felt about us being Catholic. So one day I asked the neighbors if I could go to church with them. Not only would this get me away from my family, but it would also give me a Sunday off. Perhaps, in the long run, I would be Pentecostal, and my family would be Catholic, so I could have my cake and eat it too. Had I known what I know now, I don't think I would have made such a grave mistake.

In the matter of a single Sunday morning, I learned many great things. For starters, they had taught me that the cartoons I was watching not twenty-four hours prior were Satan's propaganda; they were intended, all this time, to recruit me to the Devil's ranks. He-Man, I discovered, was entirely a slide against God and all he represented. The pastor told us that He-Man is blasphemous because he attempts to replace God by being "Master of the Universe," as the tagline goes; as we all know, God is the master of the universe, not He-Man. I believe that this was the moment in time when religious authority had stepped on my toes far too many times; they attempted to not only eliminate my leisure on Sundays, but also proselytize themselves into my Saturdays. Was nothing sacred to these inhumane cretins?

Not only did they preach about the evils found amongst the Smurf colony, but they also attempted to tell me that the music of my time was no different. ABBA was the target of this discussion. The pastor addressed "Dancing Queen" and told his congregation that when this music was played in reverse, it would produce the sounds and messages of Lucifer condemning the human population to Hell. Of course, as a child does, my curiosity got the best of me. I decided to go home that evening, and much to the confusion of my family, played "Dancing Queen" backwards on our vinyl player. If I remember as lucidly as I believe I do, the only thing that may have come out of that player was my name; well, any permutation of words that could remotely sound like my name, but that is irrelevant.

It is valid to note that at the ripe age of ten, these things being presented to me appeared to be holistically silly, even next to the universe of Rainbow Brite, which was full of strangely large-headed protagonists, white horses with rainbow hair, and spirits. The recognition that Casper the Friendly Ghost likewise wasn't real never seemed to stir me. However, it baffled me, as a child and even today, that these religious members and leaders were looking for another kind of ghost; some believed that they were even able to communicate with it. He wasn't on the television, nor was he walking on the earth, but these people insisted that he was there. All I could ever see back then and still do today when someone mentions the holy ghost is Casper, and not only did I know he wasn't real, I never would have wanted him to speak to me directly and help guide me morally and developmentally, but I knew Casper was more real than their ghost, and I was ten!

As a child of catholic parents you are required to learn all of the prayers from the Lord's Prayer, the Hail Mary, to the Apostles Creed. As any Catholic will tell you, in about the middle of the Apostles Creed it goes: "He suffered under Pontius Pilate, was crucified, died, and was buried. *He descended to the dead.* On the third day he rose again." Yet what most Catholics do not realize is that their protestant half-brothers actually say instead is *"He descended into Hell* and on the third day rose again." When I first heard this at the Pentecostal church as a ten year old I lost my mind. What was he doing in Hell, and why did the Catholics not say the same thing; who changed the words? Was he having a meeting with the devil? Was he checking to see if everything was just right for the eternal punishment of those he didn't like, was he actually the one responsible for creating Hell's art-deco, or was he just fixing the heaters? If Jesus went to Hell for three days, was it like a college Mexican long weekend piss-up or a Florida spring break relief before having to go upstairs with all that praying and worshiping and being watched by your dad for an eternity?

The question still remains: what was Jesus doing in Hell for those three days? It is remarkable that even today if you ask any religious person about these three days, they cannot give you any kind of answer and the only answers you get are complete gibberish and interpretations of scripture which have absolutely nothing to do with Hell. In Latin, the text in the Apostles Creed is "descendit ad inferos," which as you can imagine, doesn't translate to "descended to the dead." Oddly enough, Jesus hanging out in Hell for a few days does seem a little strange to even the most hardened of Christians.

Needless to say, I was more than willing to go back to Catholicism. Back then, the Catholic Church represented something more of a community rather than the terrifying religious upbringing of my misfortunate neighbor. Although my priest was relatively boring and mildly sinister looking (see current Pope Benedict XVI), he didn't often attempt to ruin my fellow peers' and my outlook on creative imaginations. And more importantly, he never tried to pry away my Saturdays, as a group of fundamentalists once said, "*from my cold dead hands.*"

This is where you begin to distinguish yourself into either the category of "religious" or "non-religious." How much are you willing to sacrifice, or compromise, in order to believe in something or someone? Well, in most people's cases, they are more than *eager* to sacrifice scientific evidence in the hopes that they will attain an eternal afterlife. They will go so far as to interpret sensory information wrongly, with the sheer intention of doing so, until it becomes a subconscious act. You can interpret anything that you choose from the Bible, and there is certain to be another interpretation that is vastly different. If you examine the Catholics and Pentecostals, one forgoes its reservations about my Saturday cartoons, while the other condemns them. Why is this? They come from the same book, with the same words, and then they commit to different ideologies in the end regardless.

The true reason that religious leaders were promoting these conspiracies was not to state *fact*, but to deride any potential intellectual influences from taking shape. Cartoons are notorious for being mindfully progressive by nature, making humorous jabs at those who fail to evaluate evolutionary evidence throughout the world, such as the "Darwin" character in *The Wild Thornberrys*, who appears as an ape who could speak and whose intelligence was superior to the protagonist. These sorts of thoughts and concepts being absorbed by children *frighten* religious leaders, as they know that it is *vital* to implant their messages into their sponge-like cerebrums. Conspiracy is what religions essentially need to survive; it's what drives them. It is second only to fear, and that is what this entire segment is about.

It is said that the two most powerful emotions that a human being can possess are both *love* and *fear*. Love is motivational in the sense that it can simultaneously teach one to protect those they love, as well as sacrifice a part or whole of themselves to promote another's well-being. It has created some of the finest pieces of artwork known in recorded history, whether it be *Romeo and Juliet*, "Something" by the Beatles, or Edgar Allan Poe's woeful *Annabelle Lee*. It has brought together individuals who have changed the course of history, with the story of Cleopatra and Mark Antony resounding strongly.

But there has always been a more prevalent sense of *urgency* in fear. It has never been said that one could wait forever to *frighten* another, nor could time slow down when fear was around. Religious leaders from within the entire spectrum of humanity have tested the limits of faith, and no other place on earth could represent the sense of fear that consumes us than "Hell." This device has plagued the minds of the religious for centuries, and it continues to be used as a metaphor for evil itself, as well as a place no sane individual would like to end up. For some, it is just another *place* that proves of little interest. However, for the devoted, it imprisons their mind and provides their motivations. Offering a pot of gold at the end of a rainbow may cause the few to follow it, but punishment for those who refuse to try will yield superior results.

This punishment for Christians for non-belief has evolved though, from the Jewish belief that there is no Hell or Devil (and let us be very clear, the Christians did evolve from the Jewish religion, but remember the Jews think that if you don't believe then who cares). You don't get their version of paradise. It wasn't until the "turn the other cheek," "love thy neighbor," peaceful magician with his "pick a card" parlor tricks decided non-belief wasn't enough and thereby required more motivation that the Christians today got what is universally known as Hell. Yet, amazingly enough, Jesus and his band of Merry Men weren't the individuals responsible for developing the original concept. We can attribute this to, at the very least, the ancient Egyptian culture. The cult of the god Osiris originally solidified the idea of eternal punishment in their judgment-based tribunal of 42 judges. From this, they determined if you were to end up in the "Two Fields," the ancient equivalent to Heaven, or the "devourer," which is known to punish those who slid against Osiris and, inevitably, annihilate the person in question.

Centuries later, through years of mythological evolution, we arrived at Hell. The vision of Hell has not changed much since its earliest roots, but the *imagery* of Hell definitely has. As with all things, imagery is contextually relevant. The society from which it originated, such as Fra Angelico's *The Last Judgment, Hell,* circa 1431 in the beginning of the Italian Renaissance, shapes and forms its own preconceptions about what Hell stands for. For Angelico, it was a place where Christ witnessed the soul's departure to its eternal fate. It is important to note that this work layers Heaven, Hell, and the Christ's throne, whereby Michelangelo's *Last Judgement* created a century afterwards, and arguably more vastly known, centers on Christ and spreads from there. The symbolism for this is as follows: for Angelico, an individual's actions are responsible for finding oneself in either Heaven or Hell; in Michelangelo's work, Christ is the centric judge.

Regardless of the time periods in which the work was completed, all imagery of Hell is intended to strike fear into the hearts and minds of those who spectate. Coincidentally, in 2008 the Pew Survey group studied the affect Hell had on the individuals within the United States[7]. The statistics found were intriguing. It appeared that people ten years ago were more easily convinced that Hell was a literal place, much as those described in folklore; in fact, only 59% of people were still convinced, down from 71% that previous decade. What could be the reasons for this occurrence? Could it be that people are becoming *more* intolerant of religious doctrine?

Naturally, the answer to these questions is "no," and to make matters worse, a very immense "no." The reason that people are becoming less convinced about the concept of Hell is not because they don't believe it exists, but because the belief of Hell is more frightening than the actual place. To put it plainly, individuals would rather believe that Hell is not real than experience the prospects of winding up there. To solidify this theory, from that same Pew Survey and the same experimental group, they found that the same individuals found the existence of Heaven to be synonymous amongst no less than 79% of said group. This is attributable to the beauty, the calm, and the sanctity of Heaven. When swallowing, it is a minor aspirin to Hell's horse pill.

This isn't the first time that the flocks have become unruly. There have been, historically, times when the mere possibility of infernal torture simply didn't do the trick. So those in charge, the religious leaders at the top, began their *inquisitions*. Since there have been a number of inquisitions in history, let's set our focus on the Spanish Inquisition. This movement, like all other inquisitions, was intended to root out all of the "non-believers" and discriminate

---

[7] Pewresearch.org

against particular nationalities (in this case, and more often than not, the Jews and the Muslims). It began in 1483, when King Ferdinand II began applying pressure on Pope Sixtus IV to remove these unwanted citizens. So began the Spanish Inquisition. When an individual was charged of heresy, they were given two options: elaborate on whom else (if anyone) was also a heretic, or be publically executed. By the end of the inquisition almost four hundred years later, 300,000[8] people had been burned or killed for being heretics in the eyes of the aristocracy, and almost that same amount had to flee Spain to escape religious persecution.

In New York City, within the last decade, a group of individuals who had connections throughout not only the city but the entirety of the United States, banded together and used similar tactics. They walk into stores, local, small, and often independently supported, and offer them "protection" in exchange for money or trades from that business. If the individual or business goes along for the ride, according to particular rules and standards proposed by the organization, they are left alone to operate. However, if they fail to adhere to these obligations, the organization harasses the individual and/or his or her family; they may go as far as to physically harm their shops, person, or take away their life. This organization is commonly called the "mafia," and their crime is called "extortion."

Of course, modern day religious organizations can't be accused of extortion in the same manner that inquisitors could have. But the same principles, albeit on a much larger scale, exist. Religious leaders are able to utilize *guilt*, supplemented by their powerful stature for their devoted followers, in the same way that a member of the mafia would use a shotgun. Their metaphorical shotgun happens to be Hell.

In order to instate Hell as a place where you would not want to be, there had to be a place to offer up that could foil it, much as Laertes and Fortinbras exist to do so in *Hamlet*. Therefore, religious leaders in the times of the Old Testament decided to fully realize the possible "Heaven." It became laborious for them to attempt to explain to those curious what Heaven may consist of; imagine an

---

[8] There are different estimations as to how many people actually did die ranging from 50,000 to 800,000 and as many Catholics like to point out only about 5,000 people were actually burned at the stake. That should make you feel better.

individual trying to explain Hawaii who had never experienced anything related to Hawaii. So they did what every strategist did: they used the term *unimaginable*. The next chapter is an attempt to coagulate the ever transient river of heavenly unimaginables.

# CHAPTER 4
## *Heaven*

*"Religion is excellent stuff for keeping common people quiet."*

*Napoleon Bonaparte*

What can be said about Heaven that has not already been conceptualized beyond necessity by nearly every human being on the Earth? Even for freethinking, non-religious members of communities, a similar "Heaven" is not often far away from their minds. It represents the perfect place; the greatest of paradises, sort of like Hawaii on steroids. But for the religious, it represents ultimate *fulfillment* in life. It is the place they work to be granted a ticket to since they were fully conscious, indoctrinated creatures. Although it is not described explicitly in the Bible, we are given some minor foundations upon which to expound. For instance, in Revelations, we are given some incredibly vague insight:

Then the angel showed me the river of the water of life, bright as crystal, flowing from the throne of God and of the Lamb through the middle of the street of the city; also, on either side of the river, the tree of life with its twelve kinds of fruit, yielding its fruit each month. The leaves of the tree were for the healing of the nations. No longer will there be anything accursed, but the throne of God and of the Lamb will be in it, and his servants will worship him. They will see his face, and his name will be on their foreheads. And night will be no more. They will need no light of lamp or sun, for the Lord God will be their light, and they will reign forever and ever.

At first glance, this sounds relatively relieving. It sounds very *fluorescent*, sort of like standing in the middle of a non-active but severely lit hospital. And the sound of water has always been fairly soothing, so only *God* knows how a river of liquid life would sound.

Then it begins to get strange. If we are to analyze these things literally, and we shall, then the tree of life corresponds directly to each month of the year, and allegedly each month has its own fruit. We can live with that, although I don't believe I would like to eat an entire *month* of the same thing; I think I would be just looking forward to the next month's fruit for half of the month, plus what about meat? There is no mention of a Bar-B-Q, a Porterhouse Steak, or Alaskan King Crab, so why do we all have to be vegetarians in Heaven? Can you imagine eating fruit all year long? I once ate too many oranges as a kid and spent the next 3 days on the toilet, so I can't imagine that this sounds like fun, but it gets even better. The one fact that I am not willing to cope with is having the name *God* permanently engrained on my forehead; I will be submissive to aging wrinkles, but a branded name is where I draw the line.

All sarcasm aside, this is one of the few instances where Heaven is actually described in full; or as it appears, in part, as there is a severe drought of "mansion," "beer fridge," "foot massage," and "E-Z recliner" among the passages of the Bible. What remains is a consistent focus on *worship*, which at the end of a long life of worship appears tedious. The pastors of my past emphasized the notion of worship to walk *through* the nightclub doors, and I shouldn't be expected to also kiss the foot of the bouncer, rub the back of the bartender, and shake the hands of the bathroom attendant for all eternity as well. The passages in the Bible, however, expect exactly that:

Whenever the living creatures give glory, honor and thanks to Him who sits on the throne and who lives for ever and ever, the twenty-four elders fall down before Him who sits on the throne and worship Him who lives for ever and ever. They lay their crowns before the throne and say: "You are worthy, our Lord and God, to receive glory and honor and power, for you created all things, and by your will they were created and have their being (Revelation 4:9).

And to elaborate:

Each of the four living creatures had six wings and was covered with eyes all around, even under its wings. Day and night they will never stop saying 'Holy, holy, holy is the Lord God Almighty who was, and is, and is to come' (Revelation 4:8).

And one more, as three is a lucky number:

No longer will there be any curse. The throne of God and of the Lamb will be in the city, and His servants will serve Him (Revelation 22:3).

Seriously, if this is what Heaven amounts to, what would be the purpose? Could it be that religious leaders have actually tricked themselves into believing the myth of Heaven, only to realize that after all the perpetual attempts to attain followers and live a thoroughly *godly* existence, they will not only make it into the Pearly Gates, but provide full service worship, massage, and servitude to God himself? This sounds rather self-defeating in my eyes, but maybe I haven't clearly understood altruism as the men-of-the-cloth have.

Another common misunderstanding is that most individuals think they know precisely how to attain the forever-coveted heavenly boarding pass. Most people believe that if you live a vaguely *righteous* life, you can slip into those doors almost unscathed. This righteousness can be come from a variety of sources. You can be the most appreciative, loving, and selfless individual on the planet Earth. Or perhaps, if you have the capital resources, you could invest and donate to third world countries that are far away from your personal standard of living. Maybe it is social work for those in need, whether it is a child without a home or with a disability. Perhaps you have a marvelous marriage from which children are loved and cared for. Any number of these can be conventionally acceptable for a *righteous* individual.

In Biblical mythology, however, these tasks would not be enough. As we have discovered, God is practically *indifferent* to the starving child in Zimbabwe, or the older relative saved from assisted living facilities. It is one thing, and one thing alone, which will give allowance to being *saved* by the Lord:

If you confess with your mouth, 'Jesus is Lord', and believe in your heart that God raised Him from the dead, you will be saved.... Unless you repent you will all likewise perish (Romans 10:9).

Which further begs the question: why the preoccupation with conventionally good deeds? All you need to do is comply with accepting that God exists, and that some fantastically impossible biological miracles occurred, and then you are in. So what is to happen for those poor individuals who exist in places Christian missionaries still haven't visited? According to this passage from Scripture, they have no place in Heaven, and cannot be saved. This leaves the other alternative, which allegedly is worse than Heaven. To further advance the argument, we have this tasteful quote:

> For it is by grace you have been saved, through faith – and this not from yourselves, it is the gift of God – not by works, so that no one can boast (Ephesians 2:8-9).

Which leads us to the next point of interest. If all else goes as planned, you need to insure that you die before the Second Advent of Christ (also known as the "return"). Although no one is particularly sure on the time frame in which this will occur, though a few insecure "self-prophets" assume they do, we can only imagine it to be soon; what, with the wars, famine, death, etc. The reason we must focus on this time frame in which one must die to go to Heaven is because Christ is *the only way* to get there. If he comes back in the "end-times," we will gladly assume he is not going back to his haven in the clouds for quite some time. This is mere speculation, of course, but for the religious, that is entirely acceptable.

David Copperfield is an active and popular magician. He has created numerous charities, most notably "Project Magic," which utilizes sleight-of-hand magic in an effort to help individuals who have disabilities, either temporary or permanent, as a form of physical therapy. Alongside David Copperfield is the ever famous Bill Gates of Microsoft, philanthropist, inventor, and declared atheist, pouring millions into the "Bill and Melinda Gates Foundation." This charity intends to provide for children who live in poverty or need. He happens to be a declared "non-believer." According to Biblical standards, both Copperfield and Gates would be sandwiched in Hell between the murderer, rapist, and poor child who bought a trendy Buddha statue in an oriental gift shop. Let's elaborate:

> Those who are victorious will inherit all this, and I will be their God and they will be my children. But the cowardly, the unbelieving, the vile, the murderers, the sexually immoral, those who practice magic arts, the idolaters and all liars – they will be consigned to the fiery lake of burning

sulfur. This is the second death (Galatians 5:19-21; 1 Corinthians 6:9-10; Revelation 21:7-8; Revelation 22:15).

It appears either incredibly hard to get into Heaven, i.e. the routes and sacrifices of the above mentioned, or tremendously easy, i.e. admitting that Jesus Christ is your personal Lord and Savior. I think we have found ourselves back at square one.

To make matters more interesting and convoluted, the actual actions of a murderer, rapist, or homosexual (I apologize for lumping the third in there, but we have to stick to Biblical standards) can be entirely forgiven if we simply ask for said forgiveness. So essentially, Jesus Christ will ignore the morally righteous life led by Bill Gates because frankly, Gates commits to actions based on his personal morality; Christ will, however, go out of his way to forgive an individual who has contributed nothing to society, ruined the lives of others, and committed innumerable sins if he asks for it. The paradoxes persist.

At the end of the day, the idea of Heaven sounds infinitely more taxing than what is universally construed. Worshipping God from sun up to... sun up sounds particularly exhausting, as you had spent your mortal life doing just that. And if my Heaven is full of past pedophiles, or those who shoplifted an entire warehouse of goods during their lifetime, then my heavenly neighbors do not offer much in the way of companionship. Heaven, in my eyes, sounds like a desolate, airy puff of isolation. If this is what the religious have to look forward to, I feel like as a freethinker and humanitarian non-believer, I have made the correct decision.

# CHAPTER 5
## *Religious Logic*

*"It may be that our role on this planet is not to worship God, but to create him."*

*Arthur C. Clarke*

In working on this chapter I did more research than any atheist should ever subject themselves to. I watched hundreds of hours of video, read Christian books on the story of Creation, went onto Christian chat sites to experience their communities, opened honest debates with people on forums, and watched a little more video. It all culminated in witnessing a man explain evolution using tools such as a jar of peanut butter, and honestly, that was one of the most *enlightening* experiences of my life. What I found from these various hours of different media was that there is almost no argument that remains remotely convincing. Sure, there are some decent arguments floating around the religious universe, but they crumble to pieces when you brush them off; it takes copious amounts of cleansing to find a few nuggets of worthwhile intellectual gold. In addition to this, the arguments rip at the seams when you bring them into the "real world," outside of what the Bible has come to show as reality. As a perfect analogy, we can look at the stereotypical "Snake-Oil" salesman; as long as you are mindless enough to accept his banter, then you will buy into his "cure-all" product.

We have come to learn that religion will give you everything you desire in the next life, but you must give everything to religion in this one; it will scratch your back, but you have to jump through rings of fire for it to scratch yours. As an organization, religion is superb at not only marketing to its target audience, but *selling* to that audience. This book wouldn't exist had it not been for the incredible ability for religion to persist on, becoming an ever omnipresent, potentially societally detrimental dilemma. Due to this pervasiveness, I have compiled a list of misnomers, fallacious arguments, and common phrases heard in Western society. These have become so engrained in our culture that you wouldn't be able to isolate them regularly; luckily for you, I have spent much time doing just that. Here are some of the most ridiculous arguments.

### If you found a watch...

*If you were walking in the desert and had stumbled upon a watch, having never seen one in any form, would you assume it occurred naturally or would you think someone made it?*

This is particularly in favor among the Jehovah's Witnesses; we can assume it's because they have it in their organization's name. Essentially, they are implying that finding something as intricate as a watch in the desert, whose parts are all orchestrating together in tandem and sequence, must be evidence that the watch had a designer. Likewise, if you had found a stone in the desert, you would *not* infer that it must have been *designed*. Naturally, no sane person would assume the watch was there all along. It is, after all, completely irrelevant to the natural formations around it. This argument, until recently, was never really debated. After all, it seems entirely logical that, as human beings, we attempt to identify elaborate designs and unnatural objects with their sources. The sun was subject to this for a long time. It went through many mythological incarnations. Today, the sun is just the *sun*. We no longer assign greater meaning to its existence, nor do we assume that it is anything but natural. So in the above scenario, let's pretend that the sun is a reference point for checking whether or not the watch *works*. After much tinkering, you may find that the sun is responsible for the clock's intricate numerals located on its face.

The argument continues on that if the watch was there in the sands of the desert all alone, and it appears to be designed, and it *also* appears to be correlated to the sun, then the sun must have been designed as well. How else would the sun be so strictly regulated? If the thought problem persists into the scientific era, how else would its position be so *ripe* for human life? If the sun were too far away, then Earth would become a frigid ball of ice. Too close, and we would be cooked over a naturally occurring charcoal grill. So there *must* have been someone in charge of this, and that someone would need to be incredibly precise and intelligent. Then, logically, knowing the error of their ways, that person must also not be *human*, and must know everything there is to know about space, time, and design.

Some very simple problems arise amidst this argument. For one, I would assume, like everyone else who stumbled upon the watch, that all of its parts were necessary. There would be no need for accessories to an accessory. I would assume they would all come together in a complex system, whose sole purpose is to make that watch tick. Time on the watch would remain the same, as well, rather than speeding up for some, or slowing down for others[9]. Its perfections are marked by its intricacies, and I would accept that. What I would continuously find after all of this is that there has to be a source. Now it is entirely dependent on chance whether or not we attribute this sort of things to something on the Earth or not. Personally, I would assume that like our ancestors, we wouldn't dwell on *why* it was there, but *how* we could use it to our greater benefit.

When someone walks up to my door, like a Jehovah's Witness, and they begin their preaching by asking me this question, I simply retort with another question: "Do you know why we get goosebumps?" If they know, or don't know, the answer is simple; we get them when we are frightened, cold, or in awe. Why is this relevant to the discussion, they may ask? Well goosebumps have no purpose for human beings anymore. They serve nothing more than as a reminder that at one time they *did*. So, unlike the perfection of the watch, we human beings are equipped with leftover, unused, and irrelevant pieces. If we had a grand designer, what would be the purpose of leaving behind unnecessary parts?

If we look at this rebuttal from an evolutionary standpoint (which most people avoid), we can see the exact reasons for why goosebumps exist. According to scientific evidence, they are a natural physiological trait inherited from our more animalistic ancestors. They actually served a purpose for them, and then when they evolved into forms relating to humans, over hundreds and thousands of years, their purposes ran out. For one, the hair follicles of the animal are surrounded by minuscule muscle[10], which retracts when subjected to

---

[9] Einstein's Theory of Relativity proved that when traveling at the speed of light, time would actually slow down for the person doing the traveling.

[10] piloerector muscles

cold or when the adrenal gland becomes active during stages of fear. The cold is warded off by the thick hair protruding outward, providing an extra layer of insulation.

In addition to cold, the adrenaline will make the hair of the animal stand on end, such as when a cat is being threatened by a dog. The rigid hair, together with the arched back and sideward stance the cat often assumes, make the cat appear much larger than it actually is. Like a feline, a human being will mirror this stance when in a position of fear or emotional anxiety; this can be seen in anyone who has ever walked down the aisle at their wedding, where they may experience goosebumps due to the overwhelming circumstances around them, or when you first sat through a terrifying film at your local theater. These things are called *functions* of goosebumps, and they can be seen even though they are now obsolete; we have not yet physically eliminated them in *whole* but in part.

This continues to beg the question of why a watchmaker would make parts obsolete at all; if they are an infallible, omnipresent deity that created the intricacies of the universe, there is no room or excuse for error. Goosebumps are not our only organs left behind by evolutionary progress, and to further our argument, we can look at what researchers refer to as "Jacob's Organ." It is located in the nose, and we share it with our animal descendants and peers; however, in mammals it remains functional. Much like goosebumps, this "organ" has become extinct, while its physical presence remains intact.

The Jacob's Organ was used in mammals (including humans) when we lacked a cohesive language, at least beyond muttering guttural noises. Its sole purpose was to detect the pheromones of another animal, and more particularly, an animal of opposite sex and same genetics. Nowadays, we use clothing and confidence to detect one another's sexual preference and nature. But when we didn't have language or style, all we could rely on were naturally occurring chemicals from one species to another. It may be trite now, but why create something so *imperfect?* Clearly we give too much credit to God, or any person who specializes in particulars (or everything, as God must), but there is almost no reason to do so, as He has created models not worth replicating. There is no point in creating a watch with a bell attachment; why go about creating man with useless pieces?

Not only is it ignorant to ignore the obvious, blatant evolutionary history our own body today has mapped out for us, but it is also ludicrous to assume that perfection invented imperfection. The logic behind this needs no explanation. To further our argument, we look to one of the more interesting spectacles as an example. There is a muscle located in our body which was originally used for gripping and manipulating objects with our feet[11]. The great apes, whose ancestors we also descended from are the perfect test subjects to see this muscle in action. It is now recorded that around 9%-20% of the human population is born without this muscle[12]. The point? Through Darwin's theory of use and disuse, human beings stopped needing to climb their way through the world at a certain point. Thus, it was mankind that led their own species to progress, much as we do in almost all social situations today. There is also a muscle in the ear called Darwin's Point, which helped our cave dwelling forefathers to move their ears to direct their hearing. It occurs in just over 10% of the population of humans as well as in 100% of current tree dwellers including our former ancestors. Junk DNA, male nipples, a third eyelid and Darwin's Point, all have no use to us today. This is all evidence of a watch made with too many obsolete, unwanted, and broken parts[13].

There are many theists who will discredit the argument that humans created their own metaphorical watches. With how perfect we biologically appear, how could it possibly be that we have come to this point on our own "free-will" (in case Biblical scholars do not understand)?    Through use and disuse, appropriation and misappropriation, and natural tendencies to move *forward*, mankind has done just that. However, we must never discount the amount of effort it took just to *survive*, nor the amount of time in which it took to adapt to one's own environment as beautifully as humanity has done.

If you were to sit on a park bench on a busy afternoon in the middle of Central Park, you would see some tremendous things. For one, the green pastures of the park were put there by *man*, and tended by man. We have taken matters into our own hands on how nature disperses itself. Walking through the park may be a variety of employed, semi-employed, and not-so-employed individuals living

---

[11] Plataris Muscle

[12] 9% Wikipedia - 20% Dr. Donahue

[13] If you are arguing with a creationist do not  talk about the appendix and that it has no use, they can argue that one down, that is why I didn't mention it.

amicability (most of the time). Around this park exist massive buildings which people move in and out of daily, as well as up and down mechanically. They have created social contracts with the owners and businesses of that building that they will, indeed, be there the next day to do whatever their occupation demands. They will be paid through a very complex monetary system; one that is recognized not only locally or regionally but *globally*, and one that has been evolving to the point of relative universality. These individuals go to and from work in machines that start at the turn of the key; their parts move in perfect sync, and propel them forward at speeds unknown to the rest of the animal kingdom. They do all of this and far more, routinely and casually, because they and their ancestors had spent so much of their time and dedication to achieving such things. To say that perfection is unachievable unless it comes from a perfect being is logically fallacious. Of course, assuming that something is perfect is equally fallacious. For instance, we know now that our solar system is in jeopardy as we speak. We have a dying star known as the Sun that, although distant, is only self-efficient for roughly four billion more years. If humanity or its ascendants live on this planet long enough to see that time, the Earth will become uninhabitable by carbon life-forms. If the Sun manages to "stay on," so to speak, we have literally astronomically small chances of avoiding some other catastrophe. Smaller events, such as tsunamis and earthquakes, show the power of chaos.

The next time you are in Switzerland, do yourself a favor and visit a *real* watchmaker and observe the passion and perfection in his or her work. You will notice that there are no extra parts which serve no purpose being built into the watches, like the balance springs used in time pieces before the 17th century which would serve absolutely no role in watches today. If you found a watch in the desert with a bunch of extra parts, prone to defects, anomalies, stoppages and breakdowns that brought with it massive physical pain by removing the unwanted parts, maybe you would assume that God had created it, and he had done a miserably poor job; much like he had allegedly done with our ancestors previously.

## Love

*You can't see love, but that does not mean that love does not exist. Just like love, God may not appear to you, but that doesn't mean he isn't there.*

Oftentimes a non-religious person will be confronted with an argument that stumps him or her. It has happened to me, and to heavyweights in the subject matter of religion, but whenever you do hear an argument which you may not be completely qualified at the moment to answer, science will come to your rescue as in the argument comparing God with Love.

Love, as far as we are concerned, is as real an entity as its counterpart fear; of course, it means different things to other people, but retains many of the core, universal properties everyone knows. Even in science, where we cannot see certain astronomical entities with the naked eye, such as a black hole, we have discovered such things using high-powered instruments.

I begin to break down the argument as follows: I love my wife, and I know she loves me. We say these things to one another, and have dedicated our lives, our marriage, and our children to one another. The way we look in each other's eyes, the way she kisses me as only she could, the gentle caress of my hand that she promotes whilst in the movie theater: All of these things remain observable acts of what she and I consider *love*. This of course, would be the wrong course of action to take in arguing against the theologian's argument. You cannot argue assumption in lieu of assumption, and we won't begin to do this here. We have actual scientific evidence to back up what we know to be love; although love is like a black hole, unobservable in plain sight, its effects on our physiological, emotional, and chemical reactions remain prevalent.

Science has shown us some incredible things about affection and love over the years. For instance, we know that *love* is a chemical process naturally occurring in the brain, rather than the heart. We may discredit this as an "Of course!" moment, but for quite some time, individuals remained in the dark on the matter. Furthermore, science has come to the realization that love is purely based on *survival*, at least from an evolutionary standpoint. Its original purpose came from the scenario of two individuals, a male and a female, hunter and protector, joining one another to help advance and populate their species. Love was the mechanism that came from this connection, as without it the male would have simply abandoned the mother and child, leading to the counterintuitive means by which they would have lessened survival expectancy[14].

Necessity may have brought them together, but it would be over a much greater time period, after much pondering from the likes of Shakespeare, Da Vinci, and any poet, artist, scientist, or curious individual, that love would take full form on a tangible level. Scientists have found that although love can produce positive side effects, such as the latter scenario, it can also induce states of irrationality or illogical behavior. Anyone who has ever fallen madly in love with an individual can remember the argument about who they may have been talking to at work that day of the opposite sex; that passion comes from the brain constricting blood flow, thus leading to abrupt changes in neural activity. It is to much dismay that we measure love by its negative effects, but unfortunately, they often provide great examples.

Love, unlike God, can be seen, studied, and measured, even though it remains on the tiniest, most subtle scales. Unfortunately, the argument from the religious side that they can see God's love as well as feel it is extremely common. What is more unfortunate is that we actually spend any time discussing the matter. It is more important to focus on arguments that have substantial implications, and although this may seem fruitless to the more advanced probers-of-the-mind, it is important because it represents the religious' fascination with logical fallacies. These are arguments to distract from what is primarily important, as when we get to the heavier arguments, theirs become infinitely more juvenile and rudimentary. It is strange how that works, is it not? Love can be, and is, put under a microscope, tested, retested and put to peer review. Anyone who has ever been in love knows that the opposite of love is not hate; it is indifference, it is the "I don't care anymore". Pretty much how the gods of the past and those of the present go about their daily business.

---

[14] I think I can see into the future: some religious person will read this quote and say that I am against homosexuality and that science has shown that it is wrong. I can see the headlines now: "Lance Gregorchuk agrees with what is written in the bible!"

## The Laws of Thermodynamics

It is a strange uncertainty as to why religious people will consistently fight *against* scientific principles; that is, until they find one that they can use to their advantage. A common argument is in favor of the application of thermodynamics. The basic structures for the laws of thermodynamics relate to energy, and to further that, the circumference in which energy can operate. Since three of these laws are less relevant to the argument posed by theists, we will focus on the second, which places limitations on how small energy (or matter) can actually become. Since the scientific principles behind thermodynamics can become quite tricky, especially for those not well-versed in scientific jargon, I as a layman have outlined the main concepts and tried to elaborate to the point of understanding, keeping the boundaries nice and taut. What I *will* note in particular is that most individuals know nothing about thermodynamics, which as we have discovered, makes things easily exploitable on behalf of creationism.

To briefly outline the ideas behind the second law of thermodynamics, we will first look at key concepts as they relate to the creationist argument. The first will be "entropy." This is a term consistently thrown around, which presents itself as more complicated than it really is. In classical thermodynamics, entropy refers to the amount of energy left in any "**closed**" system that is no longer available to effect change in that system. What will be posed by creationists is that this entropy is the cause of an "anti-ordering" process, which they claim is the root of evolutionary tendency, as evolution relies on order to achieve complexity. What we will observe is that entropy is a two-part system. One relies on order, and the other disorder in almost equal but opposite proportions.

If entropy is not in equilibrium, or remaining constant, it will increase in value until that equilibrium is met. In lieu of the energy bouncing around like atoms in a molecule, we know that some parts of entropy will maintain order, while the other in (almost) equal-but-opposite disorder. What is more importantly implied by this is the principle of *probability*. In relation to the "initial state" of something, say the initial universe, entropy refers to the probability of more paths leading to the "final state." Scientists outline this probability in the form of said order. In a scientific sense, we can see that when there is energy created that is maintaining an orderly fashion, there must also be an amount of energy which they consider "irretrievably disorderly."

To analogize this complicated process, assume that you have two dice. When you roll them in hopes of a two, you only have one path by which you can achieve this (1 and 1). In the hopes of rolling a seven, there are multiple paths (i.e. 4 and 3, 1 and 6, 5 and 2, and vice versa). Thus, the *probability* in achieving a "final state" of seven is much higher than the final state of one. So the final state of the universe, in essence, is the result of the most probable paths that the universe could have taken given the billions of atomic structures and combinations over a certain amount of time, accompanied by the millions of possible pathways that the entropy could have taken to produce the life forms we currently are familiar with. We can look at the order things must naturally fall into, as although chaotic there remain numeric parameters of possibility by which these things may operate. In other words, the chaos of the situation, the randomness of it all, is also responsible for the established order at the end of the roll.

To make matters more complicated, you have to analyze the difference of entropy between both an "open" and "closed" system. Since the closed system principles directly apply to the above concepts, we will consider the open system primarily because it relates to the creationist argument; this is where the problems become muddy. Since we now know that entropy increases (and by the sheer fact it increases we know that chaotic disorder was involved and in a specific way proportional to its increase), scientists assume that the process of increasing entropy is not incredibly *efficient*. This is because there has to be an expenditure of energy to manage to create a *change* in the system; *change* leads to mutations or variations in the system, which can help explain the macrocosmic and microcosmic, as well as the macro-evolutionary and micro-evolutionary. The variation itself comes from the fact that in an open system, variables are expected to come into effect.

Think of this open system in comparison to common closed systems experienced in a given science class; for this purpose, we will say chemistry. In the lab, you will be given only certain parameters in which things will operate. Maybe the teacher gives two chemicals, and instructs you to light them on fire and compare the physical or chemical reactions that you observe. We would call this a controlled or *limited* experiment, as there are only so many variables that are observed. Well the universe has millions of potential variables floating around in space, like that big yellow ball in the sky which produces heat so the possible results are seemingly endless.

All of this information relates to the creationist's fallacious argument that, since there is disorder at *all* within the system, the disorder results in *negative entropy*. In essence, they are referring to the idea that the disorder prevents *complexity* in an organism. Since we know the actual principles of thermodynamics, we can now tell that the creationists simply used upper-level scientific terms to sound intelligent and to attempt to prove something to the unsuspecting layman by confusing the law of thermodynamics in a closed system with one in an open system, respectively. In the end, their argument that thermodynamics runs counter to the core tenets of thermodynamics is, at best, a cheap attempt to prove a point with no scientific foundations.

What is the most disturbing is the creationists' fear that not only is there no "grand designer" to the universe's fabric, but that we may have come from *chaos*. I find this personally disturbing, not because mythology as science is a scarily real subject, but because the fact that we came from sheer probability is infinitely more fascinating than anything related to deities, the all-powerful or all-knowing. We are a result of billions, perhaps hundreds of trillions of years of cosmic gambling; we are the result of lucky sevens, and not only that, but millions upon millions of them.

### Evolution Is Just A Theory...

It only seems natural that this is the next step in our search for the theists' favorite arguments to support their religious justifications. After all, talking about the process by which actual biological evolution came to be is the next natural logical stepping stone. For as long as the theory has been posed, creationists have attempted to discredit, promote competitively with, and enforce opposition to the ideas of evolution. Scientists have almost *given up* in the debate on evolution as there are some things that are out of their control. For starters, evolution-as-fact is universally supported by the vast network of the scientific community, save a few scientists whose ulterior motives may seem clear to some but nevertheless get to be that

.0001% of authority figures religious scientists love to quote[15]. As posed in previous chapters, there has to be an incredible effort on their part to conspire against the world in order for evolution to be, in any part, fabricated.

That being said, it doesn't alleviate the problem at hand. No matter the evidence posed, creationists continue to push their terribly constructed, nearly scientifically obliterated theories on the origins of life in secular institutions throughout the world. Instead of "creation theory," as most people refer to it, they changed the name to "intelligent design" in order to fit into their growing secular environments. They expect intelligent design theory to be *taught* as science right alongside the factual, evidence-supported evolutionary theory that has been almost perfected over the last two centuries. This poses serious implications for the academic community. In science classes, children learn the roots of not only logic but critical thinking in general. If we begin to allow falsifiable evidence, not supported by any whim of reality, to be taught on par with science, then we create barriers between reason and rationality that simply cannot be tolerated.

Evolution is a theory. But evolution is a theory much like the theory of gravity, or Einstein's theory of relativity; they may be *theories* in practice, but the scientific principles behind them are supported by decades of experimentations and mathematical proofs. Sure, there will be the occasional superfluous and outlandish theorizing behind creationist mythology, but none bear any scientific rationalizing that can be applied using the scientific method, for instance. There can be no actual *proof* that the things that occurred happened to a definite circumstance. Even scientists repeatedly question their own theorizing. If I found a creationist-scientist that did the same, to any approximation, there would be no Christian mythologies to exist.

In the midst of World War II, a particular group of individuals who referred to themselves as the National Socialist party gained traction in Germany. The group's ferocious leader had a severe personal issue; he considered the Jewish populations responsible for plunging Germany and the associated nations into World War I (WW1), as he believed they were primarily in control of the economy, amidst other official duties. His name was Adolf Hitler, and his ideas

---

[15] I am obviously referring to Dr. Francis Collins Head of the Human Genome Project who sees DNA as God's plan.

resulted in what was deemed "The Final Solution." This campaign was one of the deadliest campaigns ever enacted by a military leader in recent memory. Its results: 6 million Jewish members of the European world emigrated, were shackled up in labor camps, and murdered on a mass scale.

Despite the overwhelming photographic, physical, eyewitness and verbal testimony, ranging from surviving victims to military soldiers to doctors involved in the rehabilitation, there remains *to this day* a surprising number of individuals who fail to believe that the situation, eventually labeled "The Holocaust," a universally known failure of mankind, ever happened[16]. Some believe that labeling it a "genocide" or "holocaust" is inappropriate, as the war resulted in the deaths rather than a "concerted effort" of any one party. Some believe that it simply never existed. These are individuals that will hold these beliefs until they expel their last breath. For those who lost loved ones, or parts of themselves either physically or emotionally, there remains an empty hole which truth will never fill. The idea of having another side of any story taught to children in classrooms because it is also "another theory" backed by the absolute opposite of evidence is absurd.

Although less catastrophic and immediately damaging, the theory of evolution has faced a history of persecution from religious authority, who attempt on a daily basis to ignore the obvious staring them in the face. Of course, if posed to do so, you could not get a religious man to jump off a cliff in order to disprove the *theory* of gravity; they will immediately, however, counter *any* argument posed by an evolutionary biologist. So what is responsible for this mental anomaly and horrible lack of appropriate intellectual judgment? Well, to be frank, they believe that they have the opposing evidence all located in their Bible. Let's examine some of these golden jewels.

The first theory we can examine that was initially posed by creationists can be found in multiple segments of the Bible, primarily Deuteronomy and Job[17]. This is the theory that the earth is flat. Despite the obvious, at the time, this was a serious estimation. The

---

[16] It must be noted that Pope John Paul in 1998 did apologize for their church doing nothing  really to stop the Nazis. So far Ratzinger hasn't said that like Galileo, they got what they deserved.

[17] Deuteronomy 13:7, 28:49, 28:64, 33:17.  Job 2:8, 19:4, 22:27, 33:13, 48:10, 59:13, 61:2, 65:5, 72:8. 38:13

theory existed when individuals only had physical observation by the naked eye. It took quite some time before we could actually *disprove* the theory of the pancake-Earth. To be fair, this theory was held by many more ancient, scientifically archaic cultures than that of the simple creationists. After all, judging from a distance, it appeared that the Earth could *only* be flat. Now that we have space orbiting satellites and imaging devices, we can actually *prove*, without a doubt and without complex mathematical work, that the Earth is indeed spherical.

The creationists let go of their theory quite easily. We don't see "neo-Flat Earthers" running around expounding the belief that science is quite wrong about our spherical Earth. Until science itself evolves further (as it will), we won't know absolutes. As a matter of fact, science is humble enough to avoid absolutes for the sake of *truth*. It is not often that scientists simply throw around theories for the sake of doing so. It typically takes many years of research before a theory is unleashed, only to be torn apart by their peers and redacted, then worked upon, and then let out of its cage once more. This peer review process is desperately needed in the religious community; unless you consider the various factions of religion responsible for doing just that to one another, ironically stepping aside their own ignorance and ridiculousness.

I suppose the primary issue that I have with creationists is that evolution is so well-accepted in the scientific community, as well as the growingly informed population, that it seems silly to discount it. In fact, on a micro-scale, evolution can be seen everywhere. We live in a world where people and scientists spend years manipulating genetics to get different variations of dogs. Now, this was not some divine inspiration that led them to these scientific findings. It is very simple; all they had to do was look at the DNA of several species prior to the modern canines we have as pets, and as they went down the line, they could see how equally the DNA's matched up to the various genetic mutations that came afterward. As we all know, dogs came from their ancestral wolves. This is terribly blatant, and can be proven through numerous DNA studies, fossil records, and logical inferences. We have come to utilize nature to accomplish artificial processes; we have created mutations of animals small enough to fit in Paris Hilton's handbag, and that is mightily impressive.

Not only have we actually *harnessed* evolution in the palms of our hand, but we have also been subjected to it time and time again.

As most informed individuals are aware of, influenza is a virus. By this definition, a virus cannot simply be cured by antibiotics. This is because each virus is a mutated variation of a previous virus. This is also relevant to computer systems, whereby malware viruses are forever changing their faces in order to not only go undetected, but in order to avoid being eliminated by the current methods applied by those who wipe viruses off the map. These are both examples of microevolution; one by nature, one by man[18]. This is also a perfect example of how evolutionary modes can be harmful as well as helpful.

I am lucky that I live in a small town just a few minutes away from the Neanderthal in Germany, where my family and I go often to the museum. Neanderthal man existed and is a perfect example of evolutionary history. He didn't die in a flood, nor was he invited onto Noah's infamous Ark. It is a fact that Neanderthal man also evolved from an ape like ancestor, as we have definite DNA matches of a certainty nearing 99.99%. Neanderthal man was not a human and lived long before the time the flood of Noah should have taken place, but the god of Moses must have simply *forgot* that he created Neanderthal man as well. Shorter than Homo Habilis, our forefathers, but definitely stronger, the Neanderthal shares a common ancestor and lived 300,000 to 30,000 years ago and then somehow died off; like the hundreds of thousands of other species of animals that have ever lived on this earth. We still are speculating as to what made Homo Sapien the chosen species over Neanderthal. What is known is that natural selection chose us[19].

As a minor diversion, I would like to point out that although we share almost *all* of our DNA with Neanderthal, *we* are the individuals argued to be in „God's likeness":

---

[18] As apposed to marcoevolution. Amazingly enough most Christians agree with microevolution as they can see it happen right in front of them. Dogs come from wolves and mules come from breading donkeys and horses but mankind? Impossible!

[19] Odly enough if your ancestors lived outside of Africa you share 4% of your DNA with the Neanderthal, meaning that in some point in your evolution your ancestors interbred with the Neanderthal Species. If your ancestors stayed in Africa, you share no DNA with the Neanderthal.

Then God said, "Let us make man in our image, after our likeness; and let them have dominion over the fish of the sea, and over the birds of the air, and over the cattle, and over all the earth, and over every creeping thing that creeps upon the earth." So God created man in his own image, in the image of God he created him; male and female he created them. And God blessed them, and God said to them, "Be fruitful and multiply, and fill the earth and subdue it; and have dominion over the fish of the sea and over the birds of the air and over every living thing that moves upon the earth." (Genesis 1: 26-28)

So I suppose we could argue that since Neanderthal is one of our closest ancestors, it was Neanderthal that shared God's likeness in as much as we did, just by close genetic proximity. Therefore, God must look like a strange hybrid of ape and man; sort of like Ron Perlman.

A major creationist argument, in an attempt to debunk hundreds of years of evolutionary theory, is that there is no physical evidence of evolution occurring in nature; or moreover, that there are far too many gaps in our physical evidence in order to positively conclude the theory as sound. This is an argument which no longer has any foundation, but unfortunately, still exists in some academic circles. So in order to put this to rest, I would like to reiterate the idea that the chances of a fossil record (the point of contention in this case) to exist *at all* is a "miracle" unto itself. Therefore, it is entirely fallacious to assume that just because we lack minor transitionary evidence linking one species to another in a *physical* form, does not eliminate evolutionary fossil records entirely. There is much ground to cover on the topic, both figuratively and literally, as the world is comprised of thirty-percent land, and the rest underwater. What we have found is, for lack of more appropriate terminology, a blessing.

One of the greatest things about science is that it's always getting better, and as it becomes more complicated and innovative, it expands on its databases and eliminates data that is no longer relevant. Science has answered important questions, and has enabled us to become very close to the place of human origin; it has given us the tools, we just need the intellectual ladders to climb over our walls of inhibition. Christians love to ask the question about why our great ape descendants, who we share between 95 % and 98.5% of our DNA with, are still apes, chimpanzees and orang-utans today if we evolved from similar ancestors. That is like asking why England is still a country if there are people in America and Canada today. Naturally, it takes small, very incremental variations to achieve the proper mutations vital to evolution. The transition from England to America or Canada, especially socially and genetically, is actually very simple to describe. However, the social variation between the two countries has shown to be incredible. They eat different foods, speak different dialects, and obtain different socio-economic identities. This is an example of how common ancestors can both remain the same and change dramatically.

But what is important today in the argument about having a common ancestor is that it could be falsifiable; it is true that 98.5% is still not 100%.   A few years ago the DNA sequence of the chimpanzee, another close relative of ours, was revealed. Chimpanzees, apes and orang-utans have 48 pairs of chromosomes. This is unlike humans, who have 46 pair of chromosomes: 23 from the father and 23 from the mother. You cannot *lose* chromosomes, as they do not disappear, so if we had a common ancestor, why would the apes have a different number of chromosomes then we do, they all have 24 pairs of chromosomes and we have just 23 pairs. If this is true, how could they have the same ancestor but not us humans?

This is an argument which creationists could have used and up to a few years ago we wouldn't have the answer; we might have said "we are looking into this, and we'll get back to you", or something along those lines, but it is a *problem* isn't it? We claim we have the same ancestor but we have a different number of chromosomes, and since you cannot simply lose a chromosome, the only possibility, we have discovered that we must have a "fused" chromosome, meaning that one of our ancestor's pairs of chromosomes fused somehow with another. This is a theory proposed years before finding the human genome project and the one for chimpanzees. The creationist thought that they had stumped science, but as always, scientists found on chromosome number 2 that 2 pairs of chromosomes had been merged together[20].

---

[20] Human Chromosome 2 is a fusion of two ancestral chromosomes by Alec MacAndrew; accessed 18 May 2006.

Chromosomes have markers called "centromeres" in the middle of the chromosome and "tetramers" at the top and bottom. Chromosome number 2 has a tetramer at the top, a tetramer in the middle, and a tetramer at the bottom. Between the two tetramers are centromeres[21].

As scientists discovered, since one cannot *lose* a chromosome, and all of their evidence supported the idea that we were directly related to our Great Ape ancestors, there must have been another explanation. As science is usually so good at doing, they found precisely what they were looking for: a perfect reason. We share our DNA almost entirely with our ancestors, and that is now a fact; one cannot simply deny physical and chemical evidence.

Our efforts to expand our territories in the name of scientific inquiry have not been fruitless. A very brave group of parents in the Dover school district of Pennsylvania brought a civil suit against the district for attempting to promote creationist ideas in the district. Hilariously, the material in question was called "Of Pandas and People"; less funny was that the material attempted to convince children that life was intelligently designed, of course, by a particular agent (implied as God). The parents would not stand for this, and they won the case in the District Court of Pennsylvania. The judges decided that the material was religious propaganda, and that no matter what, that it "cannot uncouple itself from its creationist, and thus religious, antecedents." One small step for man, as we say.

## *How do you get something from nothing?*

We are all keenly familiar with the story of the "Chicken and the Egg". It is routinely (and poorly) utilized in joke-form; it has been contemplated by serious philosophers in centuries past. It is one of those phrases so engrained in modern culture that the implied meaning of the question is often completely overlooked. There are numerous applications, whether it be in the realm of mathematics, logic, or philosophy. Its significance is such that great minds, such as Aristotle, Plutarch, and Hawking have contemplated it very deeply; beneath its simplicity, all have reduced the ultimate question to that

---

[21] Horvath & Willard Trend Genetics April 2007 April pg 174-81 and Proc. Nadl. Acad. Sci. USA Vol. 88, pp. 9051-9055, October 1991Genetics

of the creation of the universe, as it remains a perfect example of the circular nature of the logic.

Hawking came to the interesting conclusion that the egg must have come first. Naturally, this is something that most people could see as reasonable. The question begs the idea that the egg had to have originally come from the chicken; Hawking argues that the egg may not have originally been a chicken egg to begin with. As we know with Darwin's theory of natural selection, eggs were favored amongst the species: they provided shelter, mobility, and easy warmth for the host species. It is easy to assume that the egg inevitably gave way to the chicken, whether it be through genetic mutations along the way or some other set of "miraculous" consequence. So as we examine the creation of the universe, and the question that follows, we will maintain the concept and implications of the previous question.

At what I thought was the natural end to this chapter, I remained awake one night contemplating any of the arguments that may have been over-looked in the wake of other more concrete ideas. Then, as if nothing I had written before could hold a candle up to its flame, a question of infinite contemplation stumbled into my brain: "How can we get something from nothing?" Of course, this is a question that has been brought to the table time and time again. Since I am not a scientist, I would rather avoid the strenuous process of explain the Big Bang theory consistently posited in favor of a more abstract, teleological background; this would be, naturally, closer to the ideas I have tried to express previously. To begin the argument, we will have to first address the limitations implied by the question itself:

1) In essence, the argument that something can come from nothing can wind its way circularly; that nothing *must* have initially been something in order to produce something else.

2) No one specialization can represent the answer to the question in the fullest sense, so it seems impossible to answer it absolutely.

3) Finally, we have almost nothing in the ways of representation in other anomalies in other systems that could begin to demonstrate the *immenseness* of the creation of the universe.

Now that we have these things under our thumbs, we can move forward with a more logical inquiry.

As with all problems in logic, you must initially define the elements that you are dealing with. To begin the process, we will address exactly what "nothing" will represent in our thought problem. For instance, just because you can swing your hand in the air right now does not mean you are coming in contact with nothing. When you swipe your extremities through the air, that "nothing" you are coming in contact with are things which, although you cannot see, touch, or feel, exist on a molecular level; configurations exchanged between electrons and protons, for instance, provide structure to all things in the universe atomically. Just because you cannot see them with your naked eye does not mean you are "seeing" nothing. You cannot see the air you are breathing in to survive, but that does not mean you can't extract its oxygen. So nothingness is truly in the eye of the beholder, but broken down on a microscopic scale, you are coming in contact with millions of individual particles.

When you ask a layperson, rather than someone versed in chemical reactions and compositions, what *air* is made of , they will say immediately that it is comprised of oxygen. When asking a chemist or biologist the exact same question, they will provide you with a much different answer. Air is actually constructed of (perfect) percentages of various elements: (approximately) 78% nitrogen, 20% oxygen, and less than 1% of argon, carbon dioxide, neon, methane, helium, krypton, hydrogen, xenon, ozone, nitrogen dioxide, iodine, carbon monoxide, ammonia, and water vapor. This is important to note because it represents the error of human senses. These senses have failed us in the past (cue Biblical science), but science has presented us with the answers that, alone, we would never have conceived.

A common argument posed by Christians is that "something" cannot come from "nothing". So we address it as follows: is it so impossible to imagine that things have simply always existed? Dwelling on the idea that the chicken must have come from the egg, but also that the egg must have come from a chicken is missing the point. The chicken is here, and it is due to evolutionary biology that it has evolved to that status. The universe is in this same way amazing, in the true sense of the word, because it had come from something so infinitesimally miniscule (such as a singular atom) that we shouldn't persistently argue that the atom must have come from God.

This argument is also reminiscent of how God couldn't have created himself. Since I am always one to play the devil's advocate, I will pose a notion that is rarely heard from creationists: maybe there is a god that is greater than today's God, sort of like a hierarchy of familiar gods. For all we know, this could be "God XXV", or even "God 2.0." Such is the same idea for the universe. It could be that the universe exists because of previous universes outside of our own. This is the theory called the "multiverse", which has gained some scientific grounds since Hawking had popularized it in the past few decades. In order to save the explanation from its certain complicated doom, I will go about attempting to explain it as I have other scientific things: simply.

The main proponent to the entire theory of the multiverse is that of "singularity". Essentially, and this is something Einstein contemplated for quite some time, there is a point in a black hole where all the physical laws that we know exist today cease to be. On the other side of the black hole (being that we could potentially traverse it) is theorized to have a universe with a completely different set of physical law; this could be the absence of gravity, electromagnetism, and the like. Naturally, this remains just a theory. However today, it is picking up speed incredibly fast. It has given scientists and philosophers alike another look at what is possible in the very-unknown universe. Could you imagine the spectrum of permutations available to human creativity given that there could be a *Bizzaro world* outside of our own universe, and furthermore, capable of instigating life?

I suppose the way to conclude this argument is to address the significance of a god to begin with. Personally, I believe that he was initially created to justify the existence of human life. Much like the Egyptian god Ra, who helped shed light on the uses of the Sun (pun intended), humanity created an all-knowing, infinitely powerful persona to answer the ultimate question of the origin of humanity. As mentioned above, their theory simply misses the purpose. The use of God is no longer valid, as humanity is no longer the most important aspect of our universe. My eighth-grade English teacher once exclaimed that to end your thoughts with the quotes of another is a cop-out, or at best, laziness. I am not a man of convention, and I believe that the best way to explain my views on this is to quote the late, great Carl Sagan:

> "[w]ho are we? We find that we live on an insignificant planet of a humdrum star lost in a galaxy tucked away in some forgotten corner of a universe in which there are far more galaxies than people."

# CHAPTER 6
## *The Infallibility of the Bible*

*When I was a kid I used to pray every night for a new bicycle. Then I realized that the Lord does not work that way so I stole one and asked Him to forgive me.*

*Emo Philips*

The problem that most atheists find is that some of us are biologists, some are archeologists, some philosophers, astrologists, astrophysicists, nuclear particle physicists, mathematicians, or medical practitioners, but not one single person can be all at once. Regardless of the qualifications, the fact is that most of us have only *one* occupation or specialization in a particular field, and could not be *expected* to specialize in many or all. Because of this, an argument against the theory of God cannot be fully realized. It takes far too many individuals, across spectrums of scientific analysis and procurements, in order to discredit one particular theory holistically. To further the problem, we have gotten down to the bare fundamental questions of what is particularly behind the theory; although this shouldn't be a *problem*, per se, it represents a logical blockade. How do you denounce something that is naturally impossible to denounce? It is synonymous to discrediting the world of *Star Wars* even though we know it is fictionally, artificially created by George Lucas. The laws he created are his own; only *he* knows about their origins or physics.

Although this is the case faced by the scientific community, scientists and philosophers around the world must individually contend with all the issues surrounding the origins of the universe and all it comprises. As soon as we piece together these individual arguments into a larger patchwork argument, the closer we get to replacing a highly defunct, rudimentary theory on the creation of human life. In order to do this, highly specialized individuals in an unusually scrutinizing manner must pick these patches apart, and on my end (a philosophical one), we must first begin a logical discourse into certain, field-relevant matters.

These propositions lead us to a predicament: as someone who hasn't specialized in astrophysics, how do you know the precise science behind the birth of stars, which may be indicative of the laws pertaining to the rest of the universe in some significant way? Beyond natural curiosity, a philosopher or biologist has to use what is known to that specific scientific domain. In order to validate their argument utilizing this information, we have to place *trust* in the people who have dedicated their lifetimes to their respective fields. This information will be used to piece together the bigger picture arguments we are dealing with.

It must also be understood that as a personal issue in defending a particular argument with advanced theory, just like politics, the individual opposite you will consistently demand greater advanced information, and as your argument becomes a spider-web of evidence, leading from one intellectual node to another, the room for leniency decreases dramatically. The reason for this is that most Christian scientists or apologists are no fools; they exploit what they need to in order to discredit scientific thought. They do so in order to promote what most logicians call "poisoning the well"; if you discredit an authority, either from their position as a professional or attacking their personal character, their argument, regardless of legitimacy, looks untrustworthy. These fallacious tactics are hardly worth our time.

In the situations where an apologist *does* use said strategy, a debating atheist may find themselves backed into a corner; if they are good enough, they leave the atheist questioning their own disbeliefs. What must be noted and promoted is that *strategy* knows no bounds amongst science. As a scientist, freethinker, or even atheist, they must always find themselves in a position to question even the results of their own findings and arguments. Furthermore, there has to be a common understanding within *any* community that science may have its limitations, but inevitably and out of sheer probability, human knowledge will expand deep into the recesses of the unknown; as the scientific method exists, we use our tools and *known* knowledge to arrive at previously *unknown* knowledge. Therefore, only one methodology will rely on progress and results, whereas the other will pretend to have predicted today 2,000 and some odd years ago. To put it plainly, we may not have the answers now, but we *will*.

A few years ago in a debate on the Bible's literal accuracy, and more specifically, it's approximation of historical events, we analyzed the circumstances surrounding the Great Flood and Noah's Ark. Many of my colleagues do not debate people with crazy ideas because they think it gives those being debated justification in the realm of science or philosophy. Even *recognizing* their argument as debatable essentially gives them validity. Since they exist, however, we need to deal with them in full. I always argue with these people because I love the personal satisfaction of winning arguments. On this day, in this instance, however, I was highly unprepared for the questions brought to the table. I will give you a minor summary of the events which unfolded.

On this occasion, the individual proposed a question about the Great Flood. As a philosopher and logician, my limitations were worn on the sleeve of my suit jacket. My side of the argument was in favor of *logic* and *practicalities*, whereas he confronted me with controversy over precise geological evidence surrounding my argument. It was not that I had no actual knowledge of the evidence in question, but as a layman in geology for all intents and purposes, I failed to elaborate on, or discredit, the information presented. Unfortunately today, I am prepared for what happened then. Because of the humility I feel about the situation, I feel it only necessary to give the details I so horribly failed to deliver at the time. I will try to document what occurred and what was said as accurately as my recollection can procure.

We will start with the argument that instigated said propositions. The topic of discussion, as said before, was the Great Flood. To give some contextual background, the common argument among Christian scientists and apologists alike is that Earth is approximately 6,000 years old. Why this is relevant is because the Great Flood was postulated to have eroded what we have come to know as the Grand Canyon within this time frame. Naturally, from what we know now, this is geologically impossible. However, when arguing against mythical views of the non-mythical world, things can become inverted rather suddenly, and when presented with numbers that, although lacking a source, come to the forefront "convincingly," it is hard to counter it without hardcopy evidence. This is the question that both stupefied me and puzzled me, and looking at it today, I am ashamed that it had the effects it did:

"It is amazing how anyone, including my colleague, can look at the landscape of the Grand Canyon and not see the evidence of Noah's flood. In 2 Peter 3:5-7, the Bible says people will be willingly ignorant of the Creation, the flood, and the coming judgment of God, as obviously my colleague is. How can he explain that the Colorado River enters the mouth of the Grand Canyon at 2800 feet above sea level and exit the canyon at 1800 feet above sea level, but the highest point of the rim of the canyon is 7000 feet higher than the river?"

Initially, I asked myself: "Is this guy serious?" The Colorado River took millions of years of erosion to carve the miraculous, majestic properties of the Grand Canyon. If his theory were to be correct, common rainwater streams, after a busy day moving its bodies around on the pavement, could cause vast damage in the matter of their short presence. He can have his "6,000 Years" theory, but he cannot expect us to rationalize his 6,000 Years theory and his theory of the Colorado River as being inconsequential, or worse, irrelevant, to the geological evidence of the Grand Canyon. These facts are almost common knowledge; centuries of water have shown us some *amazing* geological manipulations. So why should we discount the Grand Canyon's evolution as something that just *happened*, as if God just tripped upon the Earth and his knee tore a massive, miles-long crater on its surface? To literally illustrate his argument, I have created a basic diagram:

Water enters the Grand Canyon at 2800 feet above sea level from a level plain.

The highest point of the Grand Canyon is 7000 feet above sea level.

Water Leaves the Grand Canyon at 1800 feet above sea level.

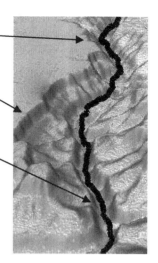

The previous information and consequent diagram is what you may come to call "hindsight," "retrospect," or "reflection." My response had almost none of the above information, even though it was already something impeccably engrained in the back of my mind. I was stumped, and being stumped was the only response I could have. A similar incident occurred to evolutionary biologist Richard Dawkins, and it will remain the only reason to put the two of us on similar ground; unless, of course, you relate our utter contempt for Christian Science and philosophy. In this case, he had his response, but it came after some contemplation. He was berated online in forums and videos for failing to respond with his usual enthusiasm; as with me, it was outside the scope of his typical expertise, and thus prompted review. Naturally, these pauses happen to any critically thinking individual. As with Dawkins, my response inevitably came, but the argument at the time appeared scientifically correct. This happens when numbers and eloquence are said in perfect sequence, allowing even ludicrous arguments to appear valid.

Here is the actual argument, leaving out the "mathematical eloquence" to its bare essentials in terms everyone may come to understand: since the Colorado River enters the Grand Canyon at 2,800 feet above sea level and exits at 1,800 feet, there can be no way that it carved out the Grand Canyon in the time Christian scientists approximate because the Grand Canyon, at its highest peak, is 7,000 feet. So as the Colorado River enters the Grand Canyon, there is no real evidence of its "grandness"; it is just a collection of simple rolling hills, over which the river casually flows. However, as the canyon opens larger and moves upward in height, you begin to notice a minute inclination. The argument goes on to pose that only a massive release of water, at one time, could have created the incline in the riverbed. He supported an argument with seemingly scientific evidence, and I commend him for doing so.

I even studied the physics behind the actions he attributes in the formation of the canyon. As it goes, whenever you have taken the beach at the ocean for granted, it is consistently defying our assumptions about gravity. Naturally, there is still a gravitational effect on the waters downwards. However, when the tide comes in, you can watch this water come onto the beach, which is usually inclined by some degree. This is why the water recedes back into the ocean as it tends to do. It is similar to when you take a paper towel and dab it in a vat of water; you can watch the water climb upwards, as its molecules bond with others. This is the essence of the science behind it. As another example, although the forces are blatantly obvious: try sucking water through a straw. It flows upwards, does it not? So the idea that water cannot flow uphill is completely false; we watch it happen every day.

Furthermore, if you look at the Colorado River from an airplane or on a map, it actually looks like the stream is going backwards, and that's because it *is*. What is now the upper Colorado River east of the Grand Canyon actually flowed in the opposite direction, fed by the Little Colorado River. The Little Colorado drained mountain highlands in eastern Arizona, ultimately draining into an inland lake in the vicinity of the present Rocky Mountains. A few million years after that, the basin-and-range country of far western Arizona formed, causing drainage to increase from the rising plateaus in the Grand Canyon region. This caused the ancestral lower Colorado River to erode heading to the east, ultimately capturing the upper Colorado River in the vicinity of the present confluence of the Little Colorado and Colorado rivers. At the same time, the rise of the Rocky Mountains disrupted the northeast flow of the Colorado River and eventually caused the river to reverse its flow. The Colorado River now flows southwest through ever deeper Marble Canyon, which is carved directly up the slope of the surrounding Marble Plateau. All the side canyons meet the river angling upstream. From the air or on a small-scale map, the effect is striking; the Colorado River is flowing the wrong way. The modern course of the Colorado

River was established about two to six million years ago. Since then, successive glacial periods followed by melting repeatedly sent large volumes of water down the Colorado River and its main tributary, Green River, rapidly increasing its depth.

What occurred in the Grand Canyon was "stream capture," which is essentially the process that occurs when a stream diverts from its own trajectory, creating a secondary stream. This takes an incredible amount of time. However, it accelerates the process of erosion by creating more streams on a greater surface area. This is what was scientifically responsible for the Grand Canyon's existence; however, there is great evidence that supports a mass amount of water as well. But when debating Christians, they naturally tend to isolate the segments of particular works, even their own Bible; by doing this, they ignore elemental facts that are also crucial, but more often than not, counter to their proposal. Let's take a paper from Ed Stiles, who is a geologist from the University of Arizona, called "Is the Grand Canyon A Geologic Infant?" My colleague attempted to attribute this source article without "Geologic" in the title. Stiles was arguing that it happened a few hundred thousand years ago, and that the Colorado River made the Grand Canyon and that it took time, but that time was minor on the geological scale of the planet. During the end of the last ice age, which happened during the Pleistocene era 110,000- 10,000 BCE, lots of water melted, sometimes very quickly, and broke off and released massive amounts of ice. It had nothing to do with God a few thousand years ago. By negating this significant fact, they were able to skew the ideas presented toward their own agendas, negating the scientific facts *actually* presented.

To discuss Noah's flood one must look no further than simple math. I married a math teacher so I know what I am talking about here. Generally, I like to use philosophy in my arguments as well as history, but if you are married to a math teacher then the only thing they understand is arithmetic and complex algorithm. Present an argument to a math teacher using mathematics, and there is no way it can be disproved. The greatest thing is that math isn't a theory; we don't have a theory of math in and of itself. So let us do some simple math to prove once again that something in the bible is not true. Why does this matter? Well, because if the story of the flood is not true, then any of the other stories may also not be true. As soon as there is *one* falsifiable incidence, like the rotten fruit ruining the whole barrel, others will follow. There is no working around the mathematics here.

We know 2+2 is 4; it is not 5, and no gods can change this basic mathematical model. In honor of mathematical principles, I thought we should break down the tale of Noah's Ark and the flood in methodical fashion. Let us begin.

In order to begin this discussion, I will first say that I am strictly avoiding the argument regarding how all of the species on the food chain became the best of cohorts on their journeys, tolerating their hunger pains *just* long enough so they could make it safely to land. I figure not only is this trite and obvious, but that it is almost a "cheap" attempt to discredit the Christian; since they have so little to argue in their favor, we will try desperately to avoid crippling an already handicapped situation. It simply too easy. We also won't consider the ideas that there are infinitely more species today than there were in the times of the proposed flood, as well as Noah's Ark. Additionally, not only is there the problem with, and the explanation for, the fish and all sea creatures as well as the mixing of salt and fresh water which would have devastating results for most if not all sea creatures, but there is also the problem with Kangaroos, Neanderthal Man, Australopithecus, and most of the animals living thousands of miles away from the middle east like penguins. I bring this up to acknowledge that I am keenly aware of these arguments, but they can be found in the numerous other books available to the public. For this book, we will focus on the mathematical laws pertaining to the already impossible scenario.

For starters, it is interesting that Noah is exactly five hundred years old; very round number, just in case someone were to mistake his birthday as the "five hundred and first." God felt compelled to destroy all of his creations, because his infallibility proved fallible. He did leave Mr. Noah behind, however. He instructed Noah to build an ark, and put two of every species of animal (in existence at the time) onto it. The ark was relative to a football field in size, and Noah was given 100 years to accomplish this task; overkill, if you were to ask a carpenter. After Noah was finished, God unleashed the waters upon the earth, flooding it to the depths. This is where "40 Days and 40 Nights" originated; it rained for the duration. Of course, this means that an *incredible* amount of rainfall had to accumulate, but that will be discussed later.

Some simple math problems can help explain the situation at hand, as well as prove that these things simply could not exist as fundamentalists see fit. Stay with me on all of this:

The earth has an average of 6371 Km radius, which is something we have known since Eratosthenes of Cyrene in the third century BCE.

So if we know the radius of something, in this case the Earth, and we want to calculate its spherical volume, most high school students have experienced the following equations:

$V = (4/3)\ \pi\ r^3$ which would give us the Volume of 1,083,206,916 kL

Genesis 7:19-20 says that the mountains were *completely* covered. We know that Mount Everest is the highest mountain in the world at 8.85 km above sea level, which would mean in order to cover the world with water to the highest point we would need to add to the radius of the earth (C=6371 km) another 8.85 km; so now we have C=6371 km+8.85 km. put those numbers into our mathematical equations of $V = (4/3)\ \pi\ r^3$ and we have a second volume of 1,087,727,260,852.17 kL. Then we take the second volume, and subtract the first volume, and we get an exact idea of how much water is needed to accomplish this goal, and that would be 4,520,344,006.42 kL.

We need to maintain our current proportions in order to contrast the gravity of the situation in terms of Noah.  If our calculations are correct, this means that if all the water which exists on the earth today was represented in your bathtub, in order to reach our projected number, you would have to fill up your bath tub a little over three times. So we are talking about more than 3 times the amount of water which is on the Earth today added to the Earth over 40 days through *rainwater*. Historically, the most rain ever recorded at one time happened in Barst Guadeloupe in 1970, and in that rainfall an amazing 1.5 inches fell to the ground in a single minute. That means if we take that number 1.5 inches multiplied by 60 minutes, whose result is multiplied by 24 (hours in a day), whose result is multiplied by the 40 days, our number would be 86,400 inches (or 219,456 CM or 2.19456 KM), which is substantially less than a quarter of the 8.85 km we need to reach the top of Everest.

Since we know the fundamentals of how science works, the science of rain is really not up for debate. The sun heats the water, it evaporates and goes to the sky (yes, just like they claim Jesus did) and comes back down (again like Jesus), but for those Christians who want to hear the particular science of precipitation, just as I would explain it to a seven year-old, here it is. This is called "The Water Cycle":

> Water droplets form from warm air. As the warm air rises in the sky it cools. Water vapor (invisible water in the air) always exists in our air. Warm air holds quite a bit of water. For example, in the summer it is usually very humid. When enough of these droplets collect together, we see them as clouds. If the clouds are big enough and have enough water droplets, the droplets bang together and form even bigger drops. When the drops get heavy, they fall because of gravity, and you see and feel rain.

Furthermore, the volume of water on earth is finite (give or take molecules). There will always be <x> million cubic kilolitres of water on Earth, though it may exist as ice, water vapor, or liquid - in lakes, oceans, and aquifers - in different fractions at any given moment. There is no rain that materializes from space, especially as it doesn't rain in space; a meteor or asteroid that had *that* much water hitting Earth could have potentially brought the missing amount of water, amidst the destruction, and yet we cannot scientifically account for said astronomical event.

To conclude the mathematical ideas behind Noah's Ark, it is clear to see that after much scrutiny, we can easily find proofs which discredit the entire concept. Unfortunately, we had to go through such efforts in order to do so. Logically, one can deduce any of this information without breaking open a high school textbook, or for that matter, an intellectual sweat. In this case, the Bible is most certainly not *infallible*; if you want to go further with this statement, this means that the individual responsible for the content of the Bible (that "God" man) is also not infallible. At the seams the Bible is bursting.

# CHAPTER 7
## *Jesus Fakes His Death*

*And if Christ be not risen, then is our preaching vain, and your faith is also vain.* (I Corinthians 15:14).

Being that the basis for this book is debate, I will tell you something that I have learned from my previous years in the field of religious, back-and-forth discussions: it is much more entertaining to debate individuals who mesh science and religion, rather than the fundamentalist who preaches all of the absolutes other than science; it is not only entertaining, but *gratifying* to see that even those who are lost to ignorance and fallacy can have a *whim* of intellectual integrity to their theories beyond what was written in an ancient book. However, the fact that this form of discourse rampages on is rather disturbing from a logical standpoint. How can a person of faith argue that the Big Bang was simply a tool used by God, a mechanism for the creation of life, and counter-intuitively argue that everything in the Bible is a historical, literal truth. This type of paradox cannot be simply thrown to the side in favor of more prominent "truths" posed by theologians, and I for one am appalled at the nature of Creationist-scientists use of *science* to support something so self-imploding. They are allowed only two options: believe that the Bible is the literal word of God, and should be followed as such, *or*, understand that the Bible is simply a device used for mythological allegory, to be taken with a grain of salt as moral anecdotes. They cannot have both.

These types of arguments come from the ancient myth that everything in the Bible is infallible. As you begin to pick the pieces apart, as we have been doing for the duration of this text and will continue to do so, you will see that this simply cannot be true. So as one part becomes impractical in terms of historical or scientific validity, the fallibility of the Bible is immediately brought into question. If a bricklayer's wall was missing a brick, and because of this, it crumbled to the ground, wouldn't you question the structural integrity of the rest of the construction? As is the case with religion; we must consistently question its structural integrity. We wouldn't need to do so if it wasn't such a prominent and influential aspect of humankind, but unfortunately, it remains so.

In the New Testament, the entirety of which relies on Jesus Christ as its central figure, we are given this missing brick on a golden tray. Corinthians offers up some of the most interesting arguments pertaining to our issues with fallibility, and it does so quite simply; we don't even need to *interpret* it beyond face-value. Here is the sentence that we will base our argument on:

> *And if Christ be not risen, then is our preaching vain, and your faith is also vain.* (15:14).

So, for those who failed to interpret this ever-revealing verse, if Christ was not resurrected, then the Christian faith and the preaching thereof is useless, moot; it is a *lie*. It is interesting that the entire foundation of Christianity rests on the shoulders of Christ dying and being resurrected. You would think that the Biblical bricklayers would have found something more sturdy and obscure, as they were so good at doing. You may be asking yourself: "Why is this so significant? Are you telling me that there are no direct loopholes to the argument?" The answer: This passage is easily one of the most significant to the cause of freethinking, scientific, and non-religious people ever. I will break it down from its historical context in the Bible all the way to the end.

In Biblical scripture, there are numerous times where it is mentioned that Christ was born in Bethlehem. Since historians have acquired new tools in order to acquire information, we have found that there is not one shred of archaeological evidence to support this. Christians, in rebuttal, argue their case based on the fact that the Roman Empire forced their citizens to return to the place of their birth, their "ancestral" city, for a census; naturally, we know that this is absolutely false. There is no record of such a thing occurring. You would assume that, after all of this time, someone in the Roman Empire would have written it down, recorded it, perhaps even *complained* about it *somewhere* in the vast documentation recovered from the era; at this point, there exists nothing and nor will there ever exist anything because it is not true. Some religious scholars argue that this was an error by the authors of the Bible. If that is the case, and the authors simply flubbed some major aspects of the Bible, then it could easily be that they did so elsewhere.

The actual reason for reporting the birthplace of Christ as being in Bethlehem is found in the Old Testament; we must remember that the New Testament was written long after the Old, and therefore, the transition between the two left massive socio-economic and logical gaps. The passage that we will concern ourselves with on this topic is found in Micah:

> But thou, Bethlehem Ephratah, though thou be little among the thousands of Judah, yet out of thee shall he come forth unto me that is to be ruler in Israel; whose goings forth have been from of old, from everlasting. (5:2)

What the Old Testament means by this passage is that the great rule of Israel is to come from Bethlehem. So when writing the New Testament, it is no surprise that this is where Matthew and Luke place Christ's birth. Luke's story is the origins of Christ's family returning to Bethlehem for the census; as a side note, this is why the story of Jesus being born in a manger exists, because as the census drew more people to Bethlehem, they had no room at the inn. In Matthew, however, the family originally lives in Bethlehem already, and Jesus is simply born there. In order to obtain the Nativity scene that we are oh-so-familiar with, these two stories need to be combined. It does seem odd though that out of all the scripture ever written, only Matthew really gets into the storytelling and make-believe. Even though the story that the **entire roman world** consisting of up to a million people could possibly be made to go to their place of birth to be counted is absurd, remember this: Matthew's story is the best of them all. The virgin birth in the manger is NEVER mentioned anywhere else in the bible, so for something pretty important to the Christian faith, like the virgin birth, is it not odd that only 2 of the gospels even mention it?

If you really analyze the context of either the gospel of Luke or Matthew, neither is supported by the reality of the first century in which they occur. In order to paint a better portrait of the events that took place, we must first create said historical context. We know today that the Roman Empire based a census around where a man worked; furthermore, they did not consider women in their census. According to Luke, Joseph lived and worked in Nazareth. Therefore, he should be taxed in Nazareth. Mary would not need to be involved at all. However, Luke writes that Joseph and (a very pregnant) Mary traveled to Bethlehem from Nazareth, and as Jesus is often referred to *as* "Jesus of Nazareth," it is hard pressing to find a reason by which we should just assume he was from Bethlehem. Especially in this time, individuals were referred to by the place they were from; i.e. "Bob of Boston." This fact alone should be enough to dismiss the Bethlehem theory, but for entertainment's sake, let's continue on with our discourse.

So now that we understand the true intent of the authors, which involved switching up some *minor* Biblical plot-points to mesh the Old and New Testament together, as well as understanding the historical pretext to the events, we can move on from this detail in order to fully antiquate a theory that is representative of an entire religion. As mentioned previously, religious scholars simply attempt to ignore these facts in light of the "bigger picture." Who is to care if Jesus was from Bethlehem or Nazareth; he still walked on water, put on elaborate David Blaine-style magic shows, and flew into the clouds upon death. Geographical location isn't going to change such miracles.

That is, until you begin to question, from the top of the tree to its roots, all the Bible has to offer. If two of the most important authors of the Bible could have potentially fabricated certain aspects of their story to satisfy important Biblical prophecies, what is to say we couldn't find other discrepancies by which to scrutinize to their very cores? What Christians need to understand is that just because something is celebrated over hundreds and even thousands of years does not mean it is true; it does not mean it is, or ever was, a real event, that ever happened. Let us continue by analyzing a favorite pastime some may know as "Easter." Yes, it happens to be the holiday that procured a magical, egg-defecating rabbit that we also devour in chocolate-shaped molds. But, as we all know, this holiday has significant religious purpose. In terms of Biblical lore, it represents the actual day that Jesus had risen after his crucifixion in order to be acquired by his Father once again. Unfortunately, we know today that this story was plagiarized from an identical story about twenty centuries beforehand, and we also know that the day that Easter was chosen has its roots in paganism, the enemy of Christianity.

First and foremost, most historians will agree that the actual day of Easter is an arbitrary date. It lands on the first Sunday after the first full moon, after the spring equinox. The pagan roots of the holiday exist in the fact that they placed great significance on astrological events. The spring equinox, as well as the winter, have been used in every significant empire for centuries, and it was no different in the past with Easter. I note this fact because this date was significant long *before* it was made the date by which Christ was resurrected. But of course it was; without a preconceived importance to the day, the authors had a far less interesting story.

This will not be discussed in detail by any Christian, as they know it doesn't say any of this information in their sacred text. But let me ask you; does this sound familiar?—Spring, flowers blooming, Easter bunnies decorating the home, Parents helping their children paint beautiful designs on eggs dyed in various colors. The eggs, which will later be hidden and searched for, are placed into lovely, seasonal Easter baskets. Forty days after abstaining from special foods will finally end the next day and the family is full of joy. The whole family picks out their best clothes to wear to the next morning's Sunday sunrise worship service to celebrate the saviour's resurrection and the renewal of life. Everyone looks forward to a pig (or ham) dinner with all the extras. It will be a great celebration day. After all, it is one of the most important religious holidays of the year.

If you guessed that this holiday was Easter, you would be very wrong. This is a description of an ancient Babylonian family—*2,000 years before Christ*—honoring the resurrection of their god, Tammuz, who was brought back from the underworld by his mother (or wife, it's sort of a fine line), Ishtar (after whom the festival was named). Ishtar was actually pronounced "Easter" in most Semitic dialects. There is no coincidence that the holiday of Ishtar sounded like Easter, occurring on the exact same Sunday that Easter does, but in Babylonia 2000 years before Christ. The coincidence is not lost upon anyone. Not only do both of these holidays coincide with one another on the same day, but they correlate themselves to specific astrological phenomena. Today the holiday in Germany is "Oestern," literally "looking east." It appears that we all have our variations, but the importance of the Christian Easter has been completely fabricated and plagiarized. This is a very significant finding, as most religious individuals believe that the holiday is original to the story of the resurrection of Christ.

And you may have thought we were actually *done* discussing Easter, but it only gets better from this point on. Not only was the date copied from more ancient cultures than that of Christ, but so was the entire portrayal of the resurrection. The work for this segment was actually done by historian James George Frazer, and he has put it together rather eloquently:

> *Now the death and resurrection of Attis were officially celebrated at Rome on the 24th and 25th of March, the latter being regarded as the spring equinox, and...according to an ancient and widespread tradition Christ suffered on the 25th of March...the tradition which placed the death of Christ on the 25th of March...is all the more remarkable because astronomical considerations prove that it can have* had no historical foundation...*When we remember that the festival of St. George in April has replaced the ancient pagan festival of the Parilia; that the festival of St. John the Baptist in June has succeeded to a heathen Midsummer festival of water; that the festival of the Assumption of the Virgin in August has ousted the festival of Diana; that the feast of All Souls [following Halloween] in November is a continuation of an old heathen feast of the dead; and that the Nativity of Christ himself was assigned to the winter solstice in December because that day was deemed the Nativity of the Sun; we can hardly be thought to be rash or unreasonable in conjecturing that the other cardinal festival of the Christian church—the solemnization of Easter—may have been in like manner, and from like motives of edification, adapted to a similar celebration of the Phyrigian god Attis at the vernal equinox...*It is a remarkable coincidence...*that the Christian and the heathen festivals of the divine death and resurrection should have been solemnized at the same season...*It is difficult to regard the coincidence as purely accidental *(The Golden Bough*, Vol. I, pp. 306-309).

Not only do we now understand that the entire foundation of a very famous Christian holiday was originally *pagan*, we can also now visualize how horribly hackneyed from previous, more creative literary practitioners, and furthermore, how the authors fabricated the entire story behind the resurrection of Jesus Christ.

Just when we would assume this would put the issue to rest, the original authors continued their relentless pursuit in nailing their own coffins shut tight. The problem exists in their very own consistencies; I know, as you should, that all of the authors are from separate time periods, whether years or decades, and their collective writings are what the New Testament is today. So although no single gospel gives an inclusive or definitive account of the resurrection of Jesus or his appearances, there are four points at which all four gospels agree:

1.  That the risen Jesus chose first to appear to women (or a woman) and to commission them (her) to proclaim this most important fact to the disciples, including Peter and the other apostles, in other words, the men were not witnesses.
2.  The prominence of Mary Magdalene in the story of the resurrection.
3.  Eye witness testimony by guards,
4.  All of the gospels contradict each other as to what actually happened.

But before we even get to the actual resurrection, let us just look at some of the facts about the death on the cross. A crucifixion was not only a showman's way to kill a man, it was also intentionally excruciating with a super-size of suffering. The Romans knew that people who would walk by and see a crucifixion would not attempt to find their way to a cross anytime soon. Though not everyone was nailed to a cross like Jesus was; some were nailed upside down, some nailed through their genitalia, while some were nailed naked so when they had to defecate, it would smear against themselves and the surrounding area, attracting insects and the like. It is important to note that the death should take a long time, and by a long time, I mean *days*. It is torture, and ask anyone who worked in Abu Garb (or the next time you are lunching with Donald Rumsfeld), and they will tell you that it is about the length of torture. So in Jesus' case, if anyone else was thinking about pretending to be the son of god, this would be a deterrent to starting your own version of Christianity. Remember, the focus is upon the idea that suffering on a cross should be something that takes some time, not hours, not minutes, but days.

Granted, there are some fanatics in the Philippines and Mexico who actually recreate the whole suffering of Jesus annually; just in case you were wondering, it is the *same* people, year after year. The get whipped, they carry a big cross, and the get nailed to it and they get hung up for hours... and they don't die, but in fact, do it again the next year. No doubt it is painful, and no doubt they suffer, but they don't die after a few hours of hanging there. Death is not the point, as they would die faster if they had their legs broken. The legs actually help hold you up, so if you break the legs, you die of asphyxiation; keep the legs unbroken and it takes a long time to die. A *very* long time. It is known in Biblical record that they left Jesus unscathed in this regard, so obviously, one would assume that they intended his death to be postponed for the sake of Jewish entertainment.

When we look at John, he gives an interesting account of the exact moment of Jesus' passing:

> *Later, knowing that everything had now been finished, and so that Scripture would be fulfilled, Jesus said, "I am thirsty." A jar of wine vinegar was there, so they soaked a sponge in it, put the sponge on a stalk of the hyssop plant, and lifted it to Jesus' lips. When he had received the drink, Jesus said, "It is finished." With that, he bowed his head and gave up his spirit.*

But what happens if that "vinegar" was actually something to render Christ unconscious, removing his ability to wake from pain and, well, crucifixion. This may seem like an elaborate conspiracy theory, but as we have come to find, nothing is what it seems about the Bible. We have seen these events occur in common pop culture, all the way from *Romeo and Juliet* to more modern cinema; people chloroform themselves for a grand number of reasons, and if you were to pull off the greatest stunt of all time (something Houdini would be jealous of), it may as well be enacted by Jesus Christ himself.

According to the Bible, however, Jesus "died" within a matter of hours. If anyone has seen *The Passion of the Christ*, the bona fide snuff film, one could reasonably assume that this could be accurate. This can be found in Mark amongst a few significant passages:

*It was the third hour when they crucified him (15:22)*

*And at the ninth hour Jesus cried out in a loud voice, "Eloi, Eloi, lama sabachthani?"—which means, "My God, my God, why have you forsaken me?" (15:34)*

So more precisely-worded, Jesus actually died after only *six* hours on the cross. Here is where things begin to get tricky. When you cross-reference this with Luke, he describes the events taking place over only *three* hours:

*It was now about noon, and darkness came over the whole land until three in the afternoon, for the sun stopped shining. And the curtain of the temple was torn in two. Jesus called out with a loud voice, "Father, into your hands I commit my spirit." When he had said this, he breathed his last (23:44-46).*

Since we know the actual purpose of crucifixion, which is an act of exhibition, a deterrent, like the days of public hanging (but infinitely more gruesome), it is very peculiar that Jesus died so suddenly. One could argue that the severity of Christ's wounds may have induced this quicker, but I personally have a different theory on the whole matter: perhaps the entire process of the crucifixion was an elaborately-staged death.

The first reaction from individuals when I propose this theory is a look of disbelief, and furthermore, a frank shrug of the shoulders and nod of the head. But when you begin to further analyse the situation at hand, we see things that at an initial glance may have been lost in scripture. For an example, a common act in crucifixion is to break the legs of those up on the cross. This insures that after the theatrical purposes of the crucifixions were fulfilled, there would be a quick and easy death so the Romans could simply move onto the next crucifixions in their agenda; the breaking of the legs led to asphyxiation, since the individual in question could obviously not support themselves by standing. However, they made sure to *not* break the legs of Jesus, as the following passage from John reads:

*The soldiers therefore came and broke the legs of the first man who had been crucified with Jesus, and then those of the other. But when they came to Jesus and found that he was already dead, they did not break his legs. Instead, one of the soldiers pierced Jesus' side with a spear, bringing a sudden flow of blood and water. The man who saw it has given testimony, and his testimony is true. He knows that he tells the truth, and he testifies so that you also may believe. These things happened so that the scripture would be fulfilled: "Not one of his bones will be broken," and, as another scripture says, "They will look on the one they have pierced (19:32-37).*

The implication of this passage is that the Roman soldier did not *want* to insure that Christ died on the cross. If that were the case, then they would have done the job swiftly. Christian scholars would argue that, in defence of this proposition, the Roman soldier did *pierce* his side with a spear, and therefore, Jesus must have died by the end of that. If I were to cross-examine this defence, I would say that based on science, this could not be possible. Why, you may ask?

We know today that when the body truly dies, a human's essential organs cease to continue working and doing their respective jobs. The heart is vital to the human body, as it circulates blood and creates its motion through pumping the blood. If Jesus had died, as the Bible had proposed, a "sudden flow of blood and water" would not have occurred, as the blood would have coagulated by this point in time. If anything, we would have a bloody cavity and minor, if any, bleeding from the wound.

Yet there remains even more important information surrounding the crucifixion, and the Bible condemns its own intents at the turn of every page. After the "death" of Jesus is pronounced, the following dialogues occurred, provided by the scripture in Mark:

*Joseph of Arimathea, a prominent ( and wealthy) member of the Council, who was himself waiting for the kingdom of God, went boldly to Pilate and asked for Jesus' body (15:43).*

*Pilate couldn't believe that Jesus was already dead, so he called for the Roman officer and asked if he had died yet (15:44).*

*When he learned from the Centurion that it was so, he gave the body to Joseph (15:45).*

To further implicate Joseph in the conspiracy theory, scripture claims that he and Nicodemus, who was a Pharisee and member of the Sanhedrin, brought to the tomb "a mixture of myrrh and aloes, about a hundred pound weight" (19:39). The alleged purpose of this journey was to embalming and proper burial of Christ. In order to clarify the gravity of this information, we will begin by explaining the two plants individually.

"Myrrh" is a resin found in the genus of spiny, thorny trees called *Commiphora*. In the times of Scripture, it was worth its weight in gold. The properties of myrrh have been characteristically associated with rejuvenation, as it increases blood-flow. In modern usage, it is used as an antiseptic in a variety of mouthwashes, toothpastes and sprays. "Aloe" is an infinitely more common ingredient utilized, like myrrh, for its amazingly natural healing abilities.

So the question now remains: if one is preparing Jesus for burial, why would they be bringing natural remedies to *heal* an individual? In Biblical times, these chemicals were used almost strictly for their antiseptic properties. So now we can only assume that they were going out of their way to revive Jesus from his self-induced comatose, as well as his wounds suffered by Roman guards. To further the probability that this situation actually unfolded, the place of the tomb was actually located in what we can only assume to be Joseph's garden.

This is Matthews's account of what happened:

> ... *some of the guards went into the city and told the chief priests everything that had happened. After the priests had assembled with the elders, they devised a plan to give a large sum of money to the soldiers, telling them, "You must say, 'His disciples came by night and stole him away while we were asleep.' If this comes to the governor's ears, we will satisfy him and keep you out of trouble." So they took the money and did as they were directed. And this story is still told among the Jews to this day (28:11-15).*

As we are certain beyond a reasonable doubt, Mathew is a bit of an exaggerator; we know he lied about the Bethlehem story, Matthew talks about the virgin birth, and he tries to justify the story that the disciples stole the body by saying people were already talking about "stealing the body."

Matthew's account involves reporting privileged conversations between priests and Pilate, and then secret ones between priests and guards that no Christian could have known about (27.62-65). How could Matthew possibly know that a secret conversation went on between the chief priests and the Pharisees who asked Pilate to seal the tomb and put a guard at it for three days and make it "secure?" Plus, the "Guard story" is not told in any other of the Gospels; just in Mathew. This claim is not even reported in Acts, where a lot of hostile Jewish attacks on the church are recorded. But Matthew actually saying that the Jews have been saying "we stole the body." The other Jews are lying, but they were not; *Matthew* was, and he is simply not very good at it. He tells a lot of stories which he makes up that were not supported by other scripture. What seems more likely? Jesus predicted he would go to heaven and that is why the body isn't there or his body was taken and put somewhere else?

After the visit from Joseph and Nicodemus, Jesus' body was magically gone. According to scripture, however, what was left was the most beloved "Shroud of Turin." Matthew was an intelligent writer and he knew precisely what he was doing when he documented the events of Christ's "resurrection." He knew that if *everything* was gone from the scene, then the public would simply assume that the tomb had been robbed; after all, the body of Christ would have been a prized possession that any real tomb raider would want in their collection. So he dictated that the Shroud was all that was left of Christ.

Furthermore, all four gospels report that women were the ones to find the tomb of Jesus empty, although the number varies from one (Mary Magdalene) to an unspecified number. According to Mark and Luke, the *announcement* of Jesus' resurrection was first made to women. According to Matthew and John, Jesus actually *appeared* first to women (in Mark 16:9 and John 20:14 to Mary Magdalene alone). Since Jewish purity laws prohibit anyone coming into contact with a dead body except the nearest male relative and women, why would you think that women were the eye witnesses to this miracle and not the men? Isn't it more likely that Jesus, Matthew and Mary had a plan?

Truth be told, when I was researching this theory that Jesus most likely faked his death it truly wasn't difficult to find collaborating evidence; not just in the Bible, but moreover in the non-Canonical Scriptures including The Pre-Markian Passion Narrative and The Gospel of Mary which contradict each other. Remarkably there is the eyewitness account in the Gospel of Peter which actually says that 2 men carried Jesus' body out of the tomb. Now these gospels are not included in the bible so many Christians read today but are nevertheless authenticated writings of early Christians.

If this was a court of law, and I was presenting the facts for the prosecution, I would do so in the following order:

1. Jesus faked his death on the cross with the help of a Centurion and Joseph of Arimathea.
2. Jesus died way too fast, in a few hours, as opposed to a few days and did not have his legs broken to ensure death like everyone else.
3. Matthew has a history of making stuff up.
4. Matthew could not have known about private conversations Pilate had with the high priest.
5. Matthew actually said *People are going to say we stole the body*; he knew people knew what his plan was.
6. Body goes missing but clothes left behind
7. Women are the first at the scene, no men, none of the male followers because they all needed an alibi

It takes an incredible servitude to Christianity to overlook these facts; I would even go as far as saying that is also takes an incredible amount of *ignorance* of the truth to override them. After examining everything that has been discussed, although it remains to be a conspiracy theory, one could easily see how Jesus Christ could have potentially staged his very own death. After all, it would be a great way to avoid persecution by all that wanted him dead, would give him tremendous notoriety, and would help explain a number of very strange contradictions found amongst scripture. It also helps support the idea that the Bible is stocked with an tremendous amount of fallible pieces. Even if a conspiracy of this grandeur would be knocked out of the sky (although I obviously consider it very solid), it goes to show that all of the minute pieces of the Bible have absolutely no structure to them whatsoever; it is as if the bricklayer simply gave up.

# CHAPTER 8
## *Young Earth, Old Earth*

*As people become more intelligent they care less for preaches and more for teachers.*

*- Robert G. Ingersoll*

Whenever you get into a discussion with an individual who believes that the Earth is a mere 6,000 years old, or perhaps that the earth may be older than that but that science has nothing to prove within the matter, the one scientific construct that is relevant is known as "carbon dating." More often than not, that individual will claim that carbon dating is only applicable within a very minimal time frame. What must be understood is that the science of carbon dating is accurate up until approximately 50,000 years before today. Since the process of explaining carbon dating is so tremendously intensive, I will try to be as concise with its principles as possible. At times, this is not as easy as I would like it to be, so bear with me.

Essentially, carbon dating consists of the following: when solar radiation strikes the Earth's atmosphere, it converts stable Carbon-12 (C-12) molecules, found in carbon dioxide, into radioactive Carbon-14 (C-14). C-14 is known to accumulate on all living organisms. So, when an animal dies, the C-14 loses two subatomic particles, and they are released back into the atmosphere as regular C-12. These two particles are what scientists study. The constrictive properties of C-14 are that its half-life (the time it takes for half of its atomic particles to reduce) is only 5,730 years. To put it simply, every 5,730 years, half the remaining C-14 remains on the animal. Eventually, there are very small trace-values of C-14, which makes it difficult to analyze (but still possible). Scientists utilize the mathematics of this deterioration to approximate the date, which is typically down to the year, the animal died, thus giving them an age.

People who do not rely on science or the scientific method (typically Christians) try to point to the fact that there have always been different levels of carbon present. What they are referring to is the different periods of time, whether natural or artificial, that the Earth's atmosphere contained inconsistently high values of carbon. This is what logicians refer to as a "red herring," whereby they are producing an argument that, although valid, is irrelevant and distracts from the true purpose of the method. They will argue, for instance, that something that died in 1850, for example, could be carbon dated much later than 1850 because the Industrial Revolution's carbon dioxide polluted any potential results with unusually high carbon levels. The fact that there was more carbon in the air may be true, but scientists could not care less about carbon dating something within the past 1 to 400 years. To see if something is 50 years old or 400 years old, there are other, simpler methods like asking people and looking at books to see what people corroborated about the event. Carbon dating is an effective tool for finding dates when the written record is not so precise.

Another argument constantly posed by creationists or religious scientists, which I will refer to as "young-Earth" propagandists, is the Magnetic-Field Argument. Essentially, they dispute the accuracy of carbon dating based upon the deterioration of the Earth's magnetic fields. The main problem with this position is not that the magnetic fields *aren't* deteriorating, as that is scientifically factual. The issue arises when they attempt to say that because of this, C-14 levels are almost non-existent, and therefore, highly inaccurate. No matter the *amount* of C-14, much like the amount of DNA at a crime scene, scientists still retain testable scientific methods unto which they can, with trace amounts of C-14, still attain invaluable data.

A common case reference made by young-Earth scientists and creationists alike is the case of the Vollosovitch mammoth. In this instance, they utilize unrealized data to support the argument that one piece of the mammoth was dated to roughly 29,500 years and another part at 44,000. This discrepancy, it turns out, was due to using the late Troy Pewe's data[22]. In this data, he describes three

---

[22] Quaternary Stratigraphic Nomenclature in Unglaciated Central Alaska By TROY L. PEWE  Geological Survey Professional Paper 862 Table 4 page 26

different mammoths, none of which relate to the Vollosovitch mammoth. So if you analyze his research, none of the dates correspond to the above. His research was also supportive of specimens found in Alaska, rather than the native Russia where the initial mammoth was found. Furthermore, if you actually take a look at the table, his carbon dating dates about 200 different items all ranging from plants from 500 years ago to dung 40,000 years in the past, and this survey says absolutely nowhere what the Christians try to make it say. No part of the article claims "one part of the Vollosovitch mammoth was this and another part was that." It's all a table. A simple search on the Internet on carbon dating being accurate will give you thousands of Christian websites and blogs which make reference to these two dates in Pewe's data, but if you read the actual research you will see that once again Christians can make up anything they want by picking and choosing the words and research they like and throwing away the rest. Christians know that if they get enough people to say it on their blogs and on the pulpit then even though the original scientists and their research never said what they wanted him to, they misquote them anyway. It then becomes a Christian fact, backed up by research from a respectable scientist. Essentially it would be like taking that last paragraph I wrote and taking out just some of the words and quoting me as saying Christian theories are right in their scientific results and I am wrong (just watch what they do with that last sentence: "Lance Gregorchuk on page 56 of his book actually admits...").

I will agree though that there are some limitations to the usage of C-14 that all scientists agree upon. For instance, oceanic specimens are impossible to carbon date. This is because unlike the above specimens, their C-14 levels can actually be *eroded* by the ocean's waters. Simply stated, the ocean contains significant dissolved carbon from limestone, which is old carbon with essentially *zero* trace elements of C-14. The marine specimens that derive their carbon from carbon reservoirs cannot be accurately carbon dated, so do not try to. It will give you false results; we know this.

Another instance involves organic matter (which fossils are not). The carbon dating is severely limited by very recent, in this case a matter of hundreds of years from today, corpses. These specimens need time to produce the appropriate C-14 molecules, and therefore, simply cannot be carbon dated. Many "Christian scientists" utilize data from living seals, for instance, to discredit the accuracy of carbon dating. To do so would be synonymous to trying to look at a fossil and measure its age with a ruler. Different methods must be used to accurately depict a life-cycle of certain specimens. In the sense of industrial carbon-spewing, the previous example of the living seals would be highly applicable. Since the organic matter is not yet fossilized, different amounts of trace carbon dioxide emitted from vehicles or machinery *could* potentially skew the results of scientific testing. We can look at fossils as having protective *shells*, that although do not literally exist, are protected by their own age and degradation to the fossil state.

There is more than just one way to radioactively date objects, but carbon dating is the most commonly used by evolutionary biologists. For example, many individuals use (occasionally inappropriately) the potassium-argon dating, also known as K-Ar dating, using their respective elemental designations. This process is usually applicable to geographic properties such as common rocks, boulders, etc. On a few occasions, young-Earth practitioners abused the method on rock formations that were a mere hundred years old, calculating them to be a few million years old. This inaccuracy comes from using the method to calculate a relatively *new* rock formation for more appropriately aged specimens. These individuals will often show data falsifiable by using an improper measurement system for the inappropriate specimen. When these same people use carbon dating on living specimens, it only goes to show their ignorance in the scientific field.

What must be understood about these methods, and in particular carbon dating, is that they are not intended to be used as a literally measure of a year, but a *carbon year*, which is an approximate year; for example, this could mean eleven months, or fourteen months. This is similar to a light year having different measurable properties than an actual year, whereas it is not a technical definition of a *year* as we see it today, but a measure of distance. Even though it is called a year, scientists do not mean 365 and ¼ days for the past 50,000 years.

When radioactive dating is used *appropriately*, fantastic results are yielded, giving us insight into a vast amount of previously unknown information. Tree rings provide one of the strongest examples. In 1964, the oldest tree in the United States was cut down in Nevada. It was 4,862 years of age. Scientists can compare the carbon dating of this tree to another specimen estimated to have lived approximately at the same time, and have entirely congruous results. Of course, in any experiment, there will be 5-10% error margins on average; these figures shall not dismay scientists. As more specimens are dated, there is an increasingly large reference base by which scientists decrease this variation.

To provide a controversial example, the Shroud of Turin, which was what Jesus Christ was allegedly wrapped in at his death, and what he was allegedly wearing when he rose from the dead, has been carbon dated on several occasions since the science originated. As the experiments persist year after year, and as other specimens are dated alongside it, more information becomes available to us. The experiments from the various sources that carbon dated the shroud resulted in a 95% certainty that it was from approximately 1260 to 1390 CE, which is obviously a time frame directly in contrast with the life of Jesus Christ. Some people have questioned not the validity of the experiment, but of the test sample, and the experiments remain in contention. The method for doing so, however, has not.

Another predicament scientists often find themselves in when attempting to date a specimen is *finding* said specimen. The reason for such incredible gaps in our fossil records (a point that Christians excitedly exploit) is because the probability for fossilization is enormously rare. The appropriate conditions must be met, and in the appropriate order of deterioration. Let's pose an example, and make it one which is moreover the norm:

A scientist is looking for a wooly mammoth in a field. The scientist will hope that, much like its cousins in India who are elephants, they practice similarly habitual actions. If he is lucky, the mammoth found itself by a watering hole. If his luck is even higher, that same mammoth found itself trapped in said watering hole. If the conditions were right that fateful date, the mammoth perished due to starvation. By a *miracle*, that mammoth failed to be foraged on or dragged away by potential predators and scavengers. It was simply left alone, untouched, for centuries. He also hopes that, by chance, no development contractors have accidentaly destroyed the mammoth with their machinery, or built over a potentially lucrative fossil pit. If all else is true, and the scientist finds an actual fossil dig-site to pursue, he must wish that the fossil remained as intact as possible for the process of identification; for all he knows, it could be small bones from a common wolf, which would not be worth his time excavating. If all of these conditions are satisfied, he can excavate the fossil, which he does so with the touch of an *angel*, so as not to completely disintegrate the remains, at which point he can analyze it in a lab.

The probability and time in which these events take place are almost impossible to explain to creationists. To be fair, this is because most individuals cannot *conceptualize* millions upon millions of years in which they had transpired. We cannot blame them for their short-sightedness, but we can attribute most of the ills related to their misunderstandings *to* this.

After a scientist goes through the process of carbon dating a specimen such as the mammoth described previously, they will go through years upon years of variable experimentation. Post-experimentation involves peer reviews within their own communities, lab testing by other reputable scientists, and questioning by the original scientist, and inevitably, publishing of the scientifically-backed information. Knowing this, when Christians attempt to discredit not only years of scientific experimentation and data as well as the findings, they are also attempting to discredit a vast network of the international scientific community. Do you remember the conspiracy theorizing previously discussed? This is a keen example. They *must* assume that not only is one scientist involved in a mass conspiracy to cover up their "actual" findings, but that the entire scientific community in relation to the project is as well.

So now, what would *you* do as a Christian who has just been scientifically backed into a corner? With this basic knowledge we have acquired over the hundreds of years of scientific evidence, we know that the Bible cannot be taken as literally, historically credible. We do know this about the Bible: it holds minor historical accuracies, such as information about certain time periods and its events, or the king that ruled a certain period; there is a little bit of astronomy; a whole lot of sorcery; and finally, a hint of alchemy. What we can argue now is that the stories have served their purpose in these areas, as well as being morally fibrous fables.

What is intended by this statement is that the Bible should *never* be involved in the realm of evolutionary biology, long-term historical records, geography, biology, astrology, physics, and all related sciences. The reason for this is clear, and I shall use an appropriate analogy: just because the boiling point of water is lower on an airplane in flight does not mean that in every other condition, the same remains to be true; that is why tea on an airplane is atrocious, but in my home, delicious. By this, I mean that scientific principles and the mathematics will never change; only the conditions in which they are applied.

The perfect example of their theoretical inaccuracies pertains to the commonly ludicrous "age of the Earth" debate posited on their end. According to Biblical science, the earth is only 6,000 years old, which was how this chapter was introduced. Through scientific measurement, we have calculated that they were slightly shy by approximately 4.44 billion years. Given their outdated methods of measurement, we will grant them some *minor* exceptions. Rarely anymore, however, will intelligent debaters, like William Craig, debate scientists on the age of the Earth. Craig is a famous Christian apologist, and one who defines the principles of Christian theology to its core. His argument for this terrible miscalculation in timely judgment is remedied by his admission that his views have *evolved*. This is common among many theologians today. When your theory proves wrong, don't attempt to *change* it; simply *adapt* scientific principles to your will.

The Catholic Church recently apologized for its persecution of Galileo based on Nicholas Copernicus' findings[23] that the Earth actually rotated around the sun. They too now see the error of their ways, albeit it being a few hundred years delayed. They have even come out and admitted that their initial text was actually *wrong*, in addition to a scientist being *right*. Additively, they have come to accept the core principles of evolutionary biology, utilizing Charles Darwin's methods of natural selection; of course, they adapted the idea to the notion that it was God's *tool* by which He created us, but I will give them kudos for at least *trying* to come to their senses.

The one final argument that must be discussed in its entirety in terms of *aging* would be that of the universe. As soon as the scientific community makes concerted steps forward in the effort of progress, the religious community follows suit with two steps in the opposite direction. Finally, certain aspects of the Big Bang theory have been rationalized, and like evolutionary theory, are accepted almost across the entirety of the community; as scientists, they remain skeptical even of their *own* ideas. However, the religious authorities have been

---

[23] In 2000 Pope John Paul did actually issue an appology to Galileo although the current Pope Ratzinger agrees with Paul Feyerabend that Galileo got what he deserved and that the vedict and punishment were justified.

relentless in their pursuit to dismantle any theory other than their own mundane, trite, and frankly, ridiculously simplistic vision of human creation.

The argument is as follows, and will *always*, with almost 99% of certainty, be brought to the table in a religious debate:

> "If the Big Bang theory is true, and all came from the Big Bang, then where did the Big Bang come from?"

And this is where we begin a cyclical, paradoxical argument about which we will not necessarily go into laborious, brash conclusions, nor drill trite, unknown details. It may seem a cop-out to the thinking man, but arguing about the existence of something that cannot be known at this precise moment is almost as despicable as arguing for something that is, out of sheer probability, silly enough to be construed as true. As freethinkers, we accept the challenge presented by the question, but will retain our humility in knowing that although we do not know the vital specifics today, we will some day in the future of humankind.

Of course, if you can't stand waiting for this moment to arise, or cannot successfully come up with a satisfactory theory to sate your scientific appetites, you are always welcome to use the back door, as we keep it unlocked for these specific purposes:

Well if we must question where the Big Bang came from, logically we must ask the question of where *God* Himself came from.

Two can play at the game of logical paradoxes. One cannot create oneself. And one cannot argue against or for this paradox. Therefore, this is why we will ignore absolutist questions of this nature.

Even given these paradoxes and loopholes, Christian theologians will retain the notion that God may not have created the Earth in seven days, but he did have a hell of a long time to do it by scientific standards. And therefore, this is precisely what he would have gone through to do it:

He first began creating not only the intricacies of the known Universe or Multiverse, but He also had to persistently create its consequent laws and all that apply to it. To do this is a monumental task, and although He is persistent, and had quite large quantities of time in which to do it, still remains questionable. After creating the universe, he then decided he needed to create a specific planet for individuals to worship Him for creating them in the first place; seems a bit silly if you ask me, as he could have bypassed the situation and built a large mirror. He then bombarded the planet with meteors, asteroids, and even other planets in order to erode its shape and orbital complexities, rather than using a godly hammer and chisel; perhaps that's what he had in mind all along. He then created, after millions of years of deciding, single-celled organisms, as just creating a stand-up human being was far too easy. God is an intricate man, if you didn't notice. The RNA and proteins of this single-celled organism made it very simple for it to mutate amongst itself, replicating and multiplying broadly to produce other single celled organisms. God grew tired of watching these mundane single-cells float around with no purpose, so he allowed them to become multiple-celled organisms. Inevitably, these kept multiplying, and eventually they turned into even more mundane organisms such as aquatic animals without limbs or eyes, to reptiles that could lick the air and wander about, to mammals capable of climbing, running on two legs, and frolicking about, to creatures that could eat one another in succession, to monstrosities we now call "dinosaurs"; He didn't like these creatures, or maybe He didn't like the position of the Earth or the dimensions by which it floated. So he came about with a massive meteor and destroyed these poor creatures; it is okay though, because they provided His experiment with plenty of fuel. Then came something resembling man, who had a fascination with sex and bananas, but God was still not satisfied. He *aborted* this particular creature in favor of another who had an infinitely "cooler" name and classification. Eventually, he got to us: Homo Homo Sapien. He favored us tremendously, even giving us free will and allowing all of us to play in a very violent, bloody sandbox in which he occasionally intervened. As soon as our brains were large enough, he even equipped us with tools by which we eradicated the very thought of Him. Not only this, but we utilized His natural enemy called *science*, by which we found nuclear weapons, the impending destruction of the Sun, a potential collision with distant asteroids and galaxies, and a severely high chance of being enveloped in a black hole.

How does that work for a master plan?

# CHAPTER 9
## *The Problem With Women*

*I distrust those people who know so well what God wants them to do because I notice it always coincides with their own desires.*

*- Susan B. Anthony*

It would be unfair to assume that religious leaders *hate* women; however, they do and have historically, the tendency to socially helotize them. Many have grown into the ideology that women are inferior, which remains commonly perpetuated within certain facets contemporary society. There remains evidence of these ideas, preserved amongst the pages and annals of legislature, which promote or directly command peremptory male behavior. For instance, in Vermont, it was previously illegal for a woman to possess false teeth without consent from her husband. Of course, this example presents a much sillier issue than the much more complex chauvinistic laws. To elaborate, a woman in Illinois had to address all bachelors by *master*, not *mister*, in the case that they were the bachelor's female counterpart.

Although these laws and customs today are considered laughable and absurd, when they were active, they had illuminated the severity of female oppression. Then the question remains, much like anything else: "Where did this intolerance come from?" Man and woman, regardless of race or nationality, have to be a cohesive unit. So what developed male chauvinism? It is now safe to say that, upon analysis, many of these rules were cultivated from religious bigotry. Religious doctrines have been historically sexist, racist, socially isolationist, and generally intolerant.

As skeptics, we must be wary of the omnipresence of male authority. When individuals attempt to persuade others, such as a politician swaying voters, they often use material that will provoke empathy, whether or not their policies do. Religious leaders operate synonymously, although behind an ideological "smokescreen" to camouflage their primeval paper trail. Some, however, operate openly; they are not afraid to display their disdain for the female population. Regardless, they provide their attendees with a dangerous form of trickery, as well as the skeptic with their religious *modus operandi*; once you are inside of the mind, lifestyles, and values of an individual, you can begin to control these elements from afar.

We consider an organization sexist if they don't allow women to be in charge, or attain equal status, within it. If a golf club were to never allow women as members, a business were to never hire a woman, or political organization never recognize the woman as a potential candidate, the social hellfire for their actions would be met with viciousness. The policies would be considered backwards, wrong, sexist, and the general population would reject them.

So why does religion, in the greatest magic show of all, completely disappear off the radar? Is it because we consider religious leaders and their subsequent cult behaviors acceptable? This question is rhetorical, as yes, they *are* commonly accepted whether or not an individual is aware. As soon as we begin to condone the various other actions of these religious sects, we unintentionally adopt their latent policies as well.

It is true, however, that religious organizations will argue that they have personally engaged the female population and promoted them to higher positions within the church, or for that matter, have actually endorsed the actions among their religious peers. However, these represent the few and far between. Catholicism, often the perpetrator of social backwardness, has for a long duration of time ignored the pleas of their feminine population, even in light of scandal. Protestants, Catholics' cousins, also retain these degradable values within their systems.

My personal favorite religious sect is the Southern Baptist Convention[24] (SBC), easily the largest Protestant community in the

---

[24] The SBC is not to be confused with the Northern Baptists who they split from in 1845 because of the issue of slavery. Guess which side they were on? It also should be noted though that the SBC did issue an apology and formally renounced their

United States, which recently condoned sexism in its most prevalent form. A fundamentalist faction (as the SBC is slightly more moderate) in May, 2000, swayed the SBC into a terrible stance. The SBC released a document, in which the following excerpt appears:

> [w]hile both men and women are gifted for service in the church, the office of pastor is limited to men as qualified by Scripture.[25]

The origins of these beliefs come from the Timothy verses found in all versions of the Bible. This is an excerpt from Timothy:

> [l]et the woman learn in silence with all subjection. But I suffer not a woman to teach , nor to usurp authority over the man, but to be in silence. For Adam was first formed, then Eve. And Adam was not deceived, but the woman being deceived was in the transgression (Timothy 2:9-14).

To translate this passage into a reasonable English format:

> The woman should be silent and submissive. She should not teach (presumably anything in relation to life), nor should she have any authority over her husband/mate/etc. Because Adam came before Eve, God intended men to have precedence. Adam did not pick the poisonous fruit; that person was Eve. Therefore, Eve is the one who was wrong.

---

position of slavery and segregation in 1995, just 150 years later. In a statement, Richard Land, a former head of the Southern Baptist Christian Life Commission, said "...slavery played a role in the formation of the SB convention and that too often we had not acted to promote racial equality, and we apologize for that. We lament that. We grieve over that and we repent of it and we ask for the forgiveness of our African-American brothers and sisters, furthermore, the commission also asked for forgiveness for Southern Baptists having failed to support the civil rights movement." Yet then again slavery was and is justified in the old and the new testament including Matthew 18:25, Mark 14:66, Luke 12:45-48, Ephesians 6:5-9, Colossians 4:1, and of course 1 **Timothy** 6:1-3. Their whole justification for women not teaching is in Timothy. So is their justification until 1995 for having slaves!

[25] http://www.sbc.net/bfm/bfm2000.asp

In other, more subtle words, a religious leader may say the above passage from Timothy, but in all reality, is simply telling woman: "Keep your mouth shut, do as you're told, and no one will get hurt."

The SBC statement continues as follows:

> ...with the issue of women in the pastorate [at this time because they] were driven by biblical authority, a sense of urgency, and the near unanimous verdict of our churches... there is no biblical precedent for a woman in the pastorate, and the Bible teaches that women should not teach authority over men. [F]ar less than one percent of churches cooperating with the Southern Baptist Convention have ever called a woman a pasture[26].

According to the United States Census Bureau, in 2011 women represent 50.9% of the population, and if we assume that they also make up 50.9% of the SBC, it seems completely ironic that they have absolutely no say in their religion. Basing a social policy or subsequent social practices on ancient scripture is ludicrous to begin with. Now we must contend with the idea of basing these things on a single passage from the Bible. To top off the absurdity, no one is certain who originally authored Timothy; although now we know for certain that Timothy himself was detestable, unless of course, the author was the detestable one. In modern society, psychologists would profile Timothy as a classic chauvinist, one who has an inferiority complex (perhaps stemming from a lack of endowment) and a totalitarian personality.

Claire Murphy, who holds a PhD in psychology, specializing in abusive dominance, runs a website called SpeakOutLoud, dedicated to aiding those who have suffered at the hands of misogyny. Remember, this website has absolutely nothing to do with religion, but male abuse. She writes:

> [m]any men who psychologically abuse and control their female partners do not define their behavior as cruel or

---

[26] http://www.sbc.net/bfm/bfm2000.asp

abusive. This is partly because their behaviours make perfect sense when viewed from their belief system – their socially reinforced belief system.

In her writing, she gives the following criteria of an abusive chauvinist:

- Men should be "top dog," the boss, the one in control.

- Women should do as the man says.

- Men are entitled to correct or discipline their partner if she strays from behaviour expected from the female partner.

- Men are entitled to define the rules.

- Women are possessions.

I think if we were to analyze and match the previous text from Timothy and from the Southern Baptist Convention, we can identify him and them identically as the character described above.

Another issue raised by the scriptures comes to light when they are analyzed deeply. Timothy may describe that women should have no power, but it also emphasizes the concept of female servitude. For instance, referencing the infamous Timothy yet again, he argues that women should "...adorn themselves in modest apparel, with shamefacedness and sobriety; not braided hair or gold or pearls or costly array..." So essentially, man or God should be given the task of dictating precisely how a woman should dress; even what she should value.

The SBC, once again without fail, further utilize this passage to their advantage. In 1998, they released a statement that said that a wife should "submit herself graciously to the servant leadership of her husband." It is now a question of whether the leaders of the SBC maintain the *silence* of the woman, or for that matter, allow them to truly participate in their worship without the predilection of being feminine. According to Timothy, according to God, they should simply keep their mouths shut.

Judges holds one of the most despicable evidences of male dominance, although this time, the authors invented extremely graphic scenarios. In these passages, they tell a story of a man who had a concubine (modern day mistress) who was unfaithful to him. She left him and went back to her parents' home. He went to get her, bringing with him his servant. He was successful, and continued on his journey with her and his servant by his side to Gibeah, as that was the place of Israelites. She had suggested Jebus, but the Jebusites weren't *kosher* enough for him, to put it crudely. As they went into Jebus, an elderly man invited them into his home. As they sat, men began to bang on the door and demand sex from his servant. Now this is where the tale becomes horrific. The old man replied:

> [b]ehold, here is my daughter and his concubine; them I will bring out now, and humble ye them, and do with them what seemeth good unto you; but unto this man do not so a vile thing. But the men would not hearken; so the man took his concubine, and brought her forth unto them; and they knew her, and abused her all night until the morning; and when the day began to spring, they let her go (19: 24-45).

First, note how this is a commonly unmentioned passage in the daily sermons of pastors. This passage is one that many Christians attempt to absolve, for it is considered "culturally particular" to the time in which it was written. This is not an excuse. There is no *virtuous* man or woman that would condone systematic rape on any moral level; why excuse it from the written text. It would benefit the Christian greatly to simply acknowledge these things as now irrelevant to the culture as they attempt to do; in doing so, they must also acknowledge the notion that the Bible is a guideline, rather than a literal truth.

So how would a Christian man justify these passages? It is not back to the aforementioned scapegoating of God's intent. God, in the eyes of the religious, is pardoned for his actions because He has the right to do unto others whatever he sees fit. He did put them there, after all. The man, inspired by God, sacrificed his innocent, virgin daughter, in order to save an entirely unfamiliar person. Perhaps living a Christian lifestyle isn't always what it's played up to be.

When I begin to imagine asking a SBC leader questions, the first that come to mind are as follows: "Do you have a wife? If so, does she wear nice things? Would you go out of your way to adorn her in expensive jewelry, pay for her salon appointments, if it meant making her happy? Is rape of said wife proper if done under God's will?" Since the answers to these questions are typically yes (leave the last), then it becomes a matter of logic. Why would you then follow any of the other tenets found in Timothy or Judges? It would amount to direct and unsurpassed hypocritical reveries if the rest were to be true to scripture and you continued to do these things for your spouse. You simply cannot take things out of context because of *convenience*; in the world of the Bible, it is a take-all or leave-all scenario.

The same logic works the other way: if a woman *can* have these things, as God has commanded them not to, then perhaps they could also, I don't know, operate and govern a house of worship? Teach amongst the flocks of God? Maybe, although this is a stretch, they could have some capacity of authority over their male counterparts. In a perfect world, this would be the self-evident truth. In a fundamentally religious world, however, this is far from reality.

When we begin to look at the Catholic Church, for instance, we can break it down to this:

1.  The Catholic Church is full of virgin men (allegedly).

2.  These virgin men dictate how other people procreate or fornicate.

3.  They also tell individuals (essentially) who they will have sex with.

4.  The logic crumbles at our feet.

Virginity, as mentioned in Judges, is a long-time virtue, a *prized possession,* in societies both old and new. It represents purity for some, opportunity for others. Some people obsess over the notion of bedding a virginal girl; tabloids accentuate the "sex-before-marriage" cliché propagated by most religious institutions. It is among these institutions that the previous situations are birthed, and it is among these organizations that we have sexually infatuated religious leaders. Other than the *actual* scenarios of sexual deviancy and immoral conduct among the Catholic hierarchy, generally, religious leaders seem to have a fetish for bringing up sexuality.

To elaborate, one of the most recognized stories in the entire history of Christianity is the Virgin Birth of Mary[27], the mother of Jesus Christ. As the mythos goes, Mary was artificially inseminated by God; of course, back in these days, they called artificial insemination "divine intervention," which rhymes when you say it right. She was roughly thirteen at this time, and was considered *pure*, perhaps because she was still untouched by a man. If you were to ask a fundamentalist Christian about the Immaculate Conception[28], they would respond keenly with the clichéd "God works in mysterious ways," or better yet, "God has the capacity to do anything He chooses." Perhaps they were wrong about young Mary all along; this is not blasphemy, this is biology.

Which leads directly into our next point: why the preoccupation with contraception? We haven't been practicing contraception for very long, but already huge advancements, both social and economic, have been made; yet the Catholics appear to be the only Christian organization staunchly against the use of contraceptive methods. Let's utilize one-time Catholic leader Pope Paul VI's statement from his 1968 encyclical *Humanae Vitae*:

Therefore We base Our words on the first principles of a human and Christian doctrine of marriage when We are obliged once more to declare that the direct interruption of the generative process already begun and, above all, all direct abortion, even for therapeutic reasons, are to be absolutely excluded as lawful means of regulating the number of children.

In 1960, only eight years previous, the Vatican *endorsed* the use of contraception for their nun missionaries in the Congo jungles. Their reasoning was that pregnancy from rape was a greater evil than contraception for a nun. And then the conundrum presented by this decision is increased when looking at rape victims *outside* the Congo, who are not afforded the privilege of contraception or medically induced abortion.

---

[27] Which is not called the Immaculate Conception and is so often confused by those of faith. The Immaculate Conception refers to the fact that Mary herself wasn't born through sex but also just magically appeared and therefore had no original sin.

[28] See above footnote; I love to actually ask the question in this way sometimes, just to see if they know their stuff. Most Christians do not.

Recently, however, Pope Benedict XVI has begun to open a campaign that, although limited, allows certain extremes to be allowed; for instance, he states that *male* prostitutes should utilize condoms "in the intention of reducing the risk of infection.". So finally, we have a religious zealot who is making painstakingly miniscule steps to social progress. This is coming from the same Pope who condemned AIDS in Africa, but deeply asserted that condoms were far worse. We can only suppose advocating for condoms for male prostitutes is directly correlated to their already "damned" status. Could you imagine if they were to take the next step in advocating *general* contraception?

From a philosophical and logical point of view, my personal answer would be no. This is not because of some fundamental, moral, Biblical rationale. It is because if individuals amongst their faith stopped procreating, where would their ranks go? They would be severely diminished if they advocated slowing down the biological factory line of religiously motivated parents. This is the true reason, purpose, and intent of the Catholic leadership.

Simone de Beauvoir, a French philosopher and activist, wrote about this problem in 1949 in *The Second Sex*:

Man enjoys the great advantage of having a god endorse the code he writes; and since man exercises a sovereign authority over women it is especially fortunate that this authority has been vested in him by the Supreme Being. For the Jews, Mohammedans and Christians among others, man is master by divine right; the fear of God will therefore repress any impulse towards revolt in the downtrodden female.

Unfortunately the Christians are not the only individuals who extend the idea that women should be subservient to man. The wearing of Buhrkas or the Hijab Head Scarf for women of the Muslim faith is not freedom of religion or religious expression. Women of Islam may pretend that they chose on their own to cover themselves up from head to toe so that no other man can see them simply because the Qur'an says it is to be. The Qur'an also says in 4:34 that you can beat your women (lightly, if it is useful) but if they return to obedience, seek not against them means (of annoyance). Surely, Allah is "Ever Most High, Most Great."

Any Muslim Man claiming that his Muslim wife or daughter is wearing a Buhrka or Hijab because they want to and are not under any threat of physical abuse is hiding behind a facade. Women are also *taught* the Qur'an, as are little girls, and they are forced to memorize 4:34; claiming that this is freedom of religion is ludicrous. This amounts to modern day spousal and child abuse. Children under the age of 18 must be protected by the law and not the freedom of religion. Anytime someone is told to do something, or even asked persuasively with the threat of physical violence, it is does not represent a choice.

The Qur'an is very clear on the role of women. Look no further than the clearest verse on the requirement of the hijab, found in Surah:

> [a]nd to say to the believing women that they should lower their gaze and guard their modesty; that they should not display their beauty and ornaments except what (must ordinarily) appear thereof; that they should draw their *khimār* over their bosoms and not display their beauty except to their husbands, their fathers, their husband's fathers, their sons, their husbands' sons, their brothers or their brothers' sons, or their sisters' sons, or their women, or the slaves whom their right hands possess, or male servants free of physical needs, or small children who have no sense of the shame of sex; and that they should not strike their feet in order to draw attention to their hidden ornaments. (24:30–31)

If you read this passage again and again, which I have, then you know that this is not up for interpretation. This verse is not something that women can choose for themselves. Men are allowed to beat their women for not following what Mohammed originally instructed, and they also must be covered up. This is not a choice and since we abide by the structures of religious intolerance in our society, a Muslim man can claim that his wife or daughter wants to do this. Not because of anything he did, but because of what he would be *allowed* to do under god.

And what about male servants free of physical needs? So I am guessing a homosexual nightclub is "okay" in the Islamic culture. Yet one of the passages in the text which bothers me the most is this one: "or small children who have no sense of the shame of sex." The shame of sex is the reason they are forced to cover themselves up; if they don't they will be full of shame, and will shame their families, and their families can beat them; well, only a little in the beginning until they obey the men again.

If we continue to tolerate this air of misogyny, we are no better than the individuals perpetrating these acts. Women are equally as significant to men as men are to women. Our evolution has guaranteed that one without the other would be impossible. The egg is fertilized by the sperm, but the sperm has nowhere to go without the egg. This universalism is what reigns supreme; mythology and its ancient, outdated texts shall no longer prosper. Society will fail to progress unless it stops this blatant sexism, hypocrisy, and female degradation cold in its soiled tracks.

# CHAPTER 10
# *HOMOSEXUALITY*

*Of all religions the Christian is without doubt the one which should inspire tolerance most, although up to now the Christians have been the most intolerant of all men.*

*Voltaire*

There are few things that infuriate a religious male more than to be confused as a homosexual. The reasons behind this are tremendously elaborate and ancient, but in contemporary society, the public has learned to accept homosexuality as an increasingly natural tendency; the reasons for which need to be reassessed. If one must consider motive, you can first look upon religious intolerance; the worst of which is consistently perpetrated by the Catholic Church. In a statement released by Pope Benedict XVI, homosexuality, in this case specifically homosexual marriage, "threaten[s] human dignity and the future of humanity itself."[29] Assessments like the latter intend to incite *fear*, rather than rationale or logical discourse. As you will come to understand, there are deeper-seated reasons for this dialogue than what appear on the surface.

But where are these individuals finding homosexuality to be a sin? I first examined these beliefs when I attended a seminar and exhibition in 2006 curated by the National History Museum, established in Oslo, Norway. The material covered was the frequency and natural tendency of homosexual behavior in wild animals. It was the first of its kind, and promoted the uncommon opinion that homosexuality occurs *naturally* in animals. The exhibit itself contained pictures, animals, and models of species prone to homosexual

---

[29] Pope speech to US bishops(AFP) – Mar 9, 2012

tendencies; these included, among other things, monkeys, apes, southern right whales, giraffes and penguins. The museum in Norway stated that one of its many aims was to "demystify homosexuality among people... we hope to reject the all too well known argument that homosexual behaviour is a crime against nature."[30] This is the point where this issue came to the forefront of my rejection of the intolerance of religion. Let's begin to analyze the actual history of the issue, as it is something not often enough scrutinized.

Homosexuality, as an *issue,* has become a more prominent figure in religious debate, and because of this, has bled its often "contentious" principles into the public domain of politics, as politics and religion are becoming forever more inseparable. Yet, there remains the question of *significance*, as homosexuality is mentioned amongst the pages of both the Old and New Testaments only a handful of times. Often enough, these passages remain *debatably* in correlation with homosexuality at best. The most infamous and least debatable passage in the Bible is the mythology of "Sodom and Gomorrah" found in Genesis.

The Old Testament provides the majority of this story, as the New Testament moreover *refers* to the situations of Sodom and Gomorrah. To make matters convoluted, Gomorrah is mysteriously never explained, so the story's appropriate title should be "Sodom"; I suppose "and Gomorrah" had a nicer ring to it. This tale concerns two of five cities that comprise "cities of the plain" (as they were situated on the plain of the Jordan River); of the five, only one was left unscathed by God's wrath: the city of Zoar. In the story, God sends three angels to Abraham, uncle of Lot (who currently resides in Sodom), and says that he will destroy the two cities "[b]ecause the cry of Sodom and Gomorrah is great, and because their sin is very grievous" (18:20). These sins refer to Sodom being a cultural epicenter of homosexuality; the biblical Castro district.

The story continues as Abraham begs God to spare the city if he were to find men reputable enough, in this case fifty. Eventually, being a masterful haggler, Abraham whittles this number down to a mere ten. God, being reasonable, sends two of the three angels to the city of Sodom, where Lot stood at its gates. Lot offers them a proposition: "your servant's house, and tarry all night, and wash your

---

[30] From my notes October 2006 quoting Petter Bockman, curator of "Against Nature?"

feet, and ye shall rise up early, and go on your ways. And they said, Nay; but we will abide in the street all night" (19:2).    Lot led the angels into his home, feeding them unleavened bread (commonly a sign of sincerity and truth). However, before the angels lay to fall asleep, a group of men surrounded Lot's house, asking "[w]here are the men which came in to thee this night? Bring them out unto us, that we may know them" (19:5); to "know someone" in this context is argued by scholars as a euphemism for "sexual conduct."

Lot, knowing that this was an irreparable sin, suggested to the angels that "[he had] two daughters which have not known man," and that the angels could "bring them out unto you, and do ye to them as is good in your eyes," and in exchange, spare the men outside (19:8). The Old Testament fails to elaborate if the angels took advantage of the initial proposal, but they did spare the men's lives; however, they left the men behind blinded. The angels told Lot they had been sent to destroy Sodom and Gomorrah. They instructed him to flee with his family and "[e]scape for thy life; look not behind thee, neither stay thou in all the plain; escape to the mountain, lest thou be consumed" (9:17). His wife then created the phrase "curiosity killed the cat," as she looked behind her; to prove a point, they turned her into a pillar of salt. The story proceeds, whereby God destroys both Sodom and Gomorrah.

This story is the most significant in the Bible, and remains the central doctrinal piece by which individuals derive their inhibitions of homosexuality. However, many scholars argue that this act by God was not *directly* a condemnation of homosexuality, although it would be foolish to look upon this story and assume otherwise. This being said, there are a few more noteworthy passages that must be examined. In the New Testament is another verse, this time from Romans. In this passage lies one of the most direct condemnations of homosexuality, and arguably, one of the principle passages that incite the overt hatred of homosexuals in the eyes of the Christian:

For this cause God gave them up unto vile affections: for even their women did change the natural use into that which is against nature: And likewise also the men, leaving the natural use of the woman, burned in their lust one toward another; men with men working that which is unseemly, and receiving in themselves that recompence [sic] of their error which was meet. Romans 1:26-27

To boil it down, God was upset because His people were worshipping one another lustfully: the created over the creator. He therefore made an example out of them and pitted their sexual desires against the same gender. It must be noted that this is the only example of women being with other women, and furthermore, being condemned for the act. Many religious leaders attribute this single passage to the idea of simple *inclinations* to commit a homosexual act as being sinful; once again, *thou shalt not covet thy neighbor*, especially if both of you are male.

Almost every time you are in discourse with a religious individual, the morality play of who is right or wrong on the practice of homosexuality surfaces. Is it natural? Does *God* permit it? Now, if you outright ask a person of faith whether their god rejects or embraces homosexuals, they will generally say the following: "According to the Bible, homosexuals are sinful, and God will send them to Hell." This is the standard Christian response. As we have analyzed above, there are very few instances where these beliefs take precedent, and yet almost every religiously debated argument involves itself with homosexuals and their sexual lifestyles.

The Christian faith allows individuals of different faiths to wed, as long as they believe in the same principles; in this instance, that just indicates that they are both under the watchful eye of Abrahamic God. This is noted in order to foil their views on homosexuality, which, as stated above, are far from promotional; according to them, presumably, homosexuals are not covered under God's heavenly insurance policy. To further complicate this premise, their argument against same-sex relations refers to is debatably reinforced by a section in Corinthians: "It is actually reported that sexual immorality exists among you, the kind of immorality that is not permitted even among the Gentiles, so that someone is cohabiting with his father's wife." In this sense, the son slept with his stepmother; moral issues aside, the argument consists of individuals having unmarried sexual partners.

Yet, what about all of the individuals in modern society who partake in premarital sex? Surely homosexuals, who are barred from same-sex marriage, are not alone. In a study conducted in 2002, surveyors took a sample of Americans and asked them if they had participated in premarital sex. Of this sample, 95% had confirmed that they, at one time, had engaged in premarital sex[31]. If we cross-

---

[31] Public Health Reports 2006 Lawrence Finer Guttmacher Institute

analyze this with individuals who are Christian (86% in 2009), there is a massive probability that Christians had engaged in premarital sexual conduct. So, to put it plainly, homosexuals are not the only individuals that engage in "sinful" acts; Christian practitioners are equally as liable. This argument cannot, especially in present society, be relevant.

Apostle Paul, writing by inspiration of the Holy Spirit, declared that homosexuals "shall not inherit the kingdom of God" (Corinthians 6: 9-10). To be more specific, he claims:

do not be deceived: Neither the sexually immoral nor idolaters nor adulterers nor men who have sex with men nor thieves nor the greedy nor drunkards nor slanderers nor swindlers will inherit the kingdom of God.

Now, this is a perfect example of Christian taking a segment of scripture out of context for their own gain. Paul explicitly includes fornicators, idolaters (nearly everyone, especially Christians), adulterers, homosexuals (exclusively male), thieves, the greedy, drunks, slanderers, and swindlers. This is a commonly quoted segment, as it does indeed include the condemnation of homosexuals somewhere within its borders. But if we are going to seriously argue in support of this statement, there needs to be some serious adjustments.

First and foremost, he goes on to mention that "and such were some of you: But ye are washed, but ye are sanctified, but ye are justified in the name of the Lord Jesus, and by the spirit of our God" (Corinthians 6:11). Therefore, although all of the aforementioned were condemned by God, there was still hope in Christ for the Corinthians, so is there hope in favor of those who drink like Irish priests, any adolescent who stole a piece of chocolate from a candy store, or even the covetous. According to the laws of the Bible, and in this case the Ten Commandments, loving your neighbor's Porsche and loving your neighbor result in the same penalties. But there is some amount of overlooked hope in the Bible, and it is consistently overwhelmed by the out-of-context teachings of Christian leaders. Anyone who utilizes an argument akin or identical to Paul's must also stop to pay attention to the idea of redemption, as this is something that is often preached but never practiced.

Handling the passages of Leviticus and Exodus in the Old Testament is much less tortuous. As an exercise in the proper use of context, ask a Christian whether or not they believe as Leviticus says in 18:22 that "A man shalt not lie with a man like he lie with a woman." If in response they retort yes (they will), then ask them two simple questions: "Have you ever had a haircut?" and "Do you enjoy football?" The answers are as follows:

In Leviticus, God said 'Ye shall not round the corners of your heads, neither shalt thou mar the corners of thy beard' (19:27). If we are to take the context of the Bible seriously and literally, this indicates that, as Christians and subscribers to the Old Testament, one must never cut one's hair nor shall he trim his beard. This goes for everyone. As for football, Leviticus also goes on to explain that "…the pig, though it has a divided hoof, does not chew the cud; it is unclean for you. You must not eat their meat or touch their carcasses; they are unclean for you" (11:7-8).

Of course, the latter statement would put you circa 1860, but regardless, this is an exercise in taking things either too literally or far out of context. Either you can lie with a man like you can lie with a women or you cannot get a haircut or play football with your kids using a pigskin; it is that simple. The same errors arrive from any individual who has worked or pushed a button on an elevator on the Sabbath. So if we must assume that God hates homosexuals, then we must assume the same for haircuts, football, and productive citizens on the weekends according to Leviticus.

Some individuals will argue that the previous arguments are moot, as their religious practices are centric only to the New Testament. What is most curious about statements from Christians is that, among all of the Apostles, Disciples, and authors that had documented the life of Jesus Christ, they never explicitly explain the logic of the covenants. To give a background of the covenants, they are essentially the means by which God had chosen to communicate to us, in order for redemption, and to guarantee eternal life in Heaven. It is a formal agreement between God and the religious community. We can look at the Bible as a covenant document. So then a significant problem arises.

In the book of Hebrews, the paraphrased scripture is as follows: For when there is a change of the priesthood, there must also be a change of the law (7:12). The former law is set aside because it was weak and useless (for the law made nothing perfect), and a better hope is introduced, by which we draw near to God (7:18). Jesus has become the guarantee of a better covenant (7:22) and because Jesus lives forever, he has permanent priesthood (7:24). Now the ministry

Jesus has received is as superior to theirs as a covenant of which he is mediator is superior to the old one, and it is founded on better promises (8:6).

Let's begin to backtrack. The *old* covenant included those made with Adam, Noah, Abraham, Moses, David, etc. The *new* covenant came about during the Messianic age where the "Law of God," promoted by Jesus, would be written upon the hearts of men:

> "'The time is coming,' declared the Lord, 'when I will make a new covenant with the house of Israel and with the house of Judah… this is the covenant I will make with Israel after that time,' declares the Lord, 'I will put my law in their minds and write it on their hearts. I will be their God, and they will be my people'" (Jeremiah 31:31-33).

By calling this covenant "new," he has, in all essence, made the first covenant obsolete. It is stated among the pages of Hebrew that "what is obsolete and aging will soon disappear" (8:13). As it states, if there is a change in *priesthood*, and Jesus is forever a part of said priesthood, who thereby replaced the previous covenants of God, and never condemned any of the homosexual population in particular, then said tenants must be abolished from logical discourse.

If we utilize this logic, then it is clear to see that Jesus Christ's laws, like the laws of the United States Supreme Court, set precedent over previous laws. The previous laws in this case are those found in the Old Testament. This makes sense for theological purposes, because in order to give power and dominance to the philosophy of Christ, he must first take precedence over past scriptures uninvolved with him. If a Christian were to argue the above in their favor, this is something they will contend with; if you sacrifice the old laws for Jesus' new laws, as must be done, then you have nothing left for the initial argument.

As skeptics, scrutinizers, and moral journalists, we as individuals must address what I will call the "double standard" of God. If we are to believe that God created every living creature, including microorganisms and so-called "inanimate" objects, we must also understand that scientific evidence supports homosexuality as a *natural* entity. If we have made it this far, we must also believe God must have given these traits to animals. If we are to mix science and religion as individuals wrongly attempt to do, then we obligatorily accept that human beings are animals. Therefore, it is a natural tendency, as animals, that human beings experience homosexuality.

It is said that the fall of man began with the free will bestowed upon him. It is also said that animals do not possess the free will that their human counterparts do. These double standards are overwrought among the pages of the Bible, in the Old and New Testament. They are the reason that religious leaders and their communities also wrongly view the homosexual population as immoral. This is why individuals must come together to fight the religious plague of intolerance.

Yet, perhaps the issue is much deeper than *intolerance*; maybe the religious leaders who criticize the homosexual lifestyle have a different agenda altogether. I am not a homosexual; I am attracted to women and my wife catches me occasionally throwing a look at other women (of course I make sure they are not my neighbors, as that would be a *sin*). However, my next door neighbor is gay, and lives together with his partner, and has been there since we moved in to our house seven years ago. We go to their house sometimes for drinks and to play pool, as they have a really fantastic billiards table downstairs; likewise, they come over to our house for margaritas and to gander at various sports.

These men are not bisexual. They are pure-bred, bona fide homosexuals. My wife and I are *heterosexual*. I didn't choose to be a straight male; I simply *am*. They also did not choose to be homosexuals. What tends to trouble me is that there are people out there who think there is a choice in the matter. I don't have to think about being straight and my neighbors don't have to think about being gay. Homosexual pornography or imagery isn't something I am particularly attracted to, nor would I want to spend my life intimately with another male.

If I suddenly began to get aroused at the sight of two men kissing, then maybe I would think that I have a preference in the decision between homosexuality and heterosexuality. Maybe I would think that because I *choose* women right now, I might actually think that homosexuality is a choice. Now imagine if I had scientific evidence backing up the fact that homosexuality is a choice; wouldn't that be amusing? It could change the course of the debate. But the overwhelming evidence on the psychology of mankind, as well as the aforementioned natural homosexual tendencies found within nature, is entirely contrary to the proposition. In fact, I have found tremendous amounts of evidence that individuals obsessed with considering it so, as well as condemning it, may have struggles with their own sexuality.

The Department of Psychology at the University of Georgia submitted their findings to the Journal of Abnormal Psychology. They titled it "Is Homophobia Associated With Homosexual Arousal?" Let's acknowledge that an important organization of the scientific community went out of their way to perform this study. These aren't your average science fiction writers. These are psychological scientists in the pursuit of objective validity and truth. Here is the abstract from the experimental studies:

*The authors investigated the role of homosexual arousal in exclusively heterosexual men who admitted negative affect toward homosexual individuals. Participants consisted of a group of homophobic men (n = 35) and a group of non-homophobic men (n = 29); they were assigned to groups on the basis of their scores on the Index of Homophobia (W. W. Hudson & W. A. Ricketts, 1980). The men were exposed to sexually explicit erotic stimuli consisting of heterosexual, male homosexual, and lesbian videotapes, and changes in penile circumference were monitored. They also completed an Aggression Questionnaire (A. H. Buss & M. Perry, 1992). Both groups exhibited increases in penile circumference to the heterosexual and female homosexual videos. Only the homophobic men showed an increase in penile erection to male homosexual stimuli. The groups did not differ in aggression. Homophobia is apparently associated with homosexual arousal that the homophobic individual is either unaware of or denies.*

If you need elaboration on how this is relevant to our discussion, look no further than the fact that males do not get aroused when they experience anxiety, fear, or complete disgust. As any man knows those emotions are precisely what causes erections *not* to happen, especially anxiety. The body reacts to the appropriate stimuli. I'll admit, there are rare exceptions, such as people who get sexually aroused during sex while being asphyxiated to near-unconsciousness, or beaten or among other dangerous conditions; these are people who have fetishes for things that normally provoke disgust, but they are a very small number of people, in the range of 1 - 2% of the general population. The primary reason for noting this is that the experiment will be in contention with most self-righteous Christians, who will argue that rare exceptions must be further accounted for. In this case, that argument is invalid.

When Leviticus said "a man shall not lay with a man as he lays with a woman," from the modern studies, in his heart, he may have been thinking about sodomizing someone from Gomorrah! Or perhaps the fact that Paul consistently harped on men sleeping with men, and that he never said women with women, is sure proof that he himself struggled through Medieval High School with his own insecurities. Pope Benedict the XVI is carrying on the tradition of the transgender, albeit in his sinister manner, and routinely has a chance to show it, with his laughable, elaborate costumes and Gucci shoes. Yet what amazes me is that when I make those comments about their religious intolerance and when I assume that they might be in sexual turmoil, and refer to scientific evidence to prove it, some people actually think I am making suggestions which couldn't be *true*! Obviously someone like evangelist Ted Haggard would never have sex with another man; oh, wait.

The argument for a *gay gene* has prompted much controversy amongst both the scientific and non-scientific communities. However, it looks like science is coming closer to defining it. A group of Korean geneticists have actually altered the sexual preferences of female mice by removing a single gene linked to reproductive behavior. Without the gene, the mice gravitated toward mice of the same sex. Those mice that retained the gene, called FucM, were attracted to male mice (FucM is short for fucose mutarotase). Likewise, it explained that female mice without FucM avoided male mice, declined to sniff male urine, and made passes at other females. So when it comes to human beings, it may be possible that, genetically, we may in the future be able to open up the brain and dig around, manipulating sexual preference. Now I will admit it is not final proof that there is a homosexual or bisexual gene, but it is a start, and unlike religious communities, scientists will continue to test their own theories for soundness.

# CHAPTER 11
# *MORMONS*

*In your hands or that of any other person, so much power would, no doubt, be dangerous. I am the only man in the world whom it would be safe to trust with it. Remember, I am a prophet!*

*Joseph Smith, Jr.*

When analyzing religions from an objective, distant point of view, parallels between every significant religion over the last 4,000 years are drawn rather distinctly. You begin examining the same stories across cultures, regions, continents and people, and each story has a slight variation on the one before; the moral of each, however, spectacularly coincide. If you were to sit down and write them in a list, you would also spectate on something very interesting, and also incredulously obvious: each story is highly implausible, but can neither be completely rationalized or lacks the proper universal physics to demystify it. So when a Scientologist stops to criticize the Roman Catholic beliefs in the healing powers of exorcism (unless of course, Hollywood has come to confuse the Scientologist), the Roman Catholics can come back and equally but oppositely criticize the use of "E-meters; to be fair, the Catholics have a great foot-hold to do so, but I digress.

Furthermore, when considering the "insanity", both clinical and figurative, presented by all religious sects, one must not go any further than your typical orthodox Christian. They believe that a man was born of a virgin, Jonah lived inside of a whale (and survived), and a talking snake somehow managed to seduce a couple of susceptible human beings into eating fruit; if I had inserted a beanstalk that climbs to the Heavens, would you have even second guessed it? Mormonism is the newest Christian religion, and one that has shown its broadest colors in the last century. It is also one of the more intriguing Christian religions as it has developed into a particularly odd Abrahamic branch; consider it the branch that is full of leaves, but those leaves don't necessarily match the rest of their nearby neighbors. The story of the Mormons is rather long, but one particular story must be told to understand that its roots had a rather paranoid, schizophrenic, and humble beginning. That is the story of Joseph Smith, Jr..

On September 11th, 1857, a caravan of emigrants, labeled the "Fancher-Baker" party from the east coast of the United States headed west. As with similar explorers, their journey was treacherous, laborious, and incredibly taxing. Their party was comprised of men, women, and children. The destination in mind: prosperity in California. Some of these individuals were searching for a place to settle, as the east had become overpopulated in the urban areas (the place by which to make a living); some wanted tangible prosperity from the California gold rush, and some simply wanted to take their agricultural expertise from the east in order to monopolize the west. Unfortunately, none of these dreams were realized. On this fateful day, an assembly of Mormon Church members and hired-gun Native Americans happened to cross paths with the caravan.

What culminated is what many refer to today as the "Mountain Meadows Massacre" on September 7th. It began first as a group of Mormons masquerading as Native Americans (perhaps to transfer responsibility). They began assaulting the caravan, by which point the caravan took shelter in a circular embankment. They fortified themselves with their own wagons and supplies, depleting their ammunition over a four day warzone between the Native Americans and the guised Mormons. On the 11th, two Mormon militiamen then approached the caravan in order to make a deal with their respective leaders. They offered the caravan protection throughout the valley if they traded over their entire supply of livestock, food, and general supplies to the Native Americans; these are the same individuals they were cohorts with. As reasonable individuals, they complied without much hesitation. As soon as the trade commenced, the caravan felt comfortable enough to come from their fortifications. At this point, the Mormon militiamen turned back toward the men of the Fancher party and shot them in cold blood.

According to Mormon sources, which by this point are obscured by their mere implication in the events, the militiamen ordered the Native Americans to murder the women and children immediately after the demise of the male members. They left only 17 members, all of which were children, alive. They were inevitably deemed too underdeveloped to recollect the events, and so were taken in by several Mormon missionaries. The corpses left from the massacre were either dug shallow graves or left on the open ground. The significance of this event is grave, but is only the beginning to an incredibly long story behind Mormonism and its subsequent culture.

At the time of the massacre, Brigham Young, the successor to the "Prophet" Joseph Smith, was the President of the Latter-Day Saints, a name that came to be soon after his incumbency. His association with the massacre is to this day disputed by scholars, but the Church attempts to give him an alibi: his letter telling his followers to let the travelers pass arrived a few days too late. The significance placed on Young as an important spiritual guidance to the Mormon culture cannot be left untouched, but the focus of this chapter is intended to be on Joseph Smith exclusively. After we dissect the history of Smith and the founding of the Church, it is Young who will show us the origins of many modern day Mormon teachings and practices. His nickname, being the "American Moses", is reason enough to grant him some explanatory observation.

As a starting-off point, I believe that Joseph Smith was an incredibly talented con artist, and by way of his own excessive talent, was able to analyze the work done by previous religious icons and replicate them seamlessly. If you begin to break down the religion of the Latter-Day Saints, you see very familiar parallels with the Abrahamic religions of the centuries past. Much as the writers of the Testaments of the Bible, they were inspired by folklore from ancient civilizations that had come before them. In many ways, I would argue that these cultures created what became religious allegory with the intent of preserving ancient tradition; the bastardization of these ideals eventually led to what we now know as modern religion.

Joseph Smith's intentions were worn on the sleeves of his jacket. Many contemporary critics of Smith censured him openly in newspapers, public forums and debates, and much of the public resorted to calling him a "confidence man". Since it is a relatively dead phrase, I will go through the process of elaborating: it is a man (or woman) that gains the confidence and trust of another individual or group of individuals, and abusing that trust, manipulates, lies, steals, or swindles that individual or group of individuals. Using this definition, the framework for the thesis of this chapter is laid out. Smith created an elaborate scheme from the very second that he pronounced his "prophetic" visions, and plagiarized whole concepts and, as we will see, full manuscripts from others. In this patchwork ideology, Smith found a story that resonated very well with the right people. It is because of this tactic that Mormonism is one of the fastest growing religions in the 21st century, with followers internationally professing their commitment to it.

A more concise historical background is necessary to understand the actual story of the Book of Mormon. In order to set the stage, I will begin by explaining exactly where "Mormon" came from, as well as the Church's explanation for how the book came to be. As an objective, ethical, and educated process of collecting information, by the end of it, I couldn't actually believe many of the religious constructs being flung around the spiritual atmosphere by the LDS Church; they were often times more shocking than those found in common Protestant, Catholic, and Southern Baptist communities, and on occasion, even those unbelievable Scientologists.

The Book of Mormon was edited by none other than a man named Mormon. Mormon was a "prophet-historian", and was the primary editor of the entire text. He was a member of the "Nephites", which were allegedly one of four groups of early, ancient American settlers approximated about 589 BCE (none of the archaeological, scientific, or various ethnographers have corroborated their story), right alongside the "Lamanites", "Jaredites", and "Mulekites". The primary story is about the fall of the Nephites, which the Book of Mormon paints out to have been a once righteous society that had "fallen into a state of unbelief and awful wickedness". The Nephites are then wiped out by their closest relatives, the Lamanites, roughly 800 years later. Knowing what we do today, it is easy to understand that these tribes of people never existed. The Smithsonian Institute went as far as releasing a statement in direct opposition to the Book of Mormon in 1997:

> "[We have] never used the Book of Mormon in any way as a scientific guide. Smithsonian archaeologists see no direct connection between the archaeology of the New World and

the subject matter of the book… no inscriptions using Old World forms of writing have been shown to have occurred in any part of the Americas before 1492 except for a few Norse rune stones [as they were the first colony from the East to settle in America] which have been found in Greenland".

Yet, as scientists and freethinkers alike, we are never surprised to see these findings surface after a couple centuries of intellectual and scientific development. As anthropologists broaden their intellectual brushstrokes to cover cultures from an amazingly rich societal landscape, they continuously add to our banks of knowledge. So even though we have numerous incidences where Biblical and Mormon stories never add up (even when their pseudo-scientific ventures attempt to do just that), it is our job to juggle the ridiculous job of perpetual probing. We will continue to do just that.

The Mormons have an angel named Moroni. He is the son of Mormon, and considered by Smith to be the last prophet to have contributed to the Book of Mormon. According to Church lore, Moroni placed golden plates that were engraved with Old World writings (assumed to be an Egyptian variant), with their significance being that they are technically the only reputable source of the Book of Mormon passed onto Smith from Moroni, who as mentioned before belonged to Nephi, and therefore, Smith had become the next in the line of prophets endowed with the sacred information of what would become the Book of Mormon.

Many people from this point in the story actually know the rest of it, as pop culture giants *South Park* and various other humorous outlets have skewered it so well. Naturally, there should be skepticism of these sources as they have a tendency to subvert certain scenarios for the sake of entertainment. To reinforce the information presented to you in that format, however, I will discuss the precise procedure Smith undertook in order to be able to translate the plates. First and foremost, he spent year after year attempting to *obtain* the plates, which we can only assume going through the process of creative writing, gold smelting, and subsequent engraving, but that would simply reveal a bias; sense we are playing the devil's advocate, we will continue on assuming that these events are perfectly normal. According to the accounts provided by the LDS, Smith was unable to obtain the plates originally because he had set them down in order to hide them once they had been transferred to his position, which was in direct opposition to Moroni's advice; that being that Smith must hold onto them indefinitely.

So after numerous reports of supernatural activity, and annual visits to the site, he was able to procure the ever elusive golden plates. Then he had the predicament of translating the plates, because as mentioned above, they were engraved hieroglyphics. Being a fairly persistent, determined twenty-four year old (when they still existed), Smith spent almost a full year breaking down the Egyptian symbols and then, with the help of his friend and financier, Martin Harris, a highly superstitious landowner, he dictated a 116 page manuscript; this was either lost to the winds or the terribly disorganized Harris. Smith found them to be irrelevant to the completion of the Book of Mormon, or perhaps simply didn't like the story they had crafted, so he continued on with his project. It must be noted that the same events were eventually transcribed, but from an entirely different point of view, that of Nephi, which comprises book one. Furthermore, Smith claimed at the time that his adversaries would simply expect a word-for-word reiteration of the events chronicled initially, and if he didn't match those words, then they would think him fraudulent; to be fair, I would have been equally as paranoid as Smith.

In order to translate the whole book, he used what Mormon scholars like to refer to as "seer stones". These stones were not exclusive to Smith, however; the Church claims that many people in Smith's era used them to obtain revelations from God in what appears to be a fairly frequent occurrence. Today, we think of seer stones as we would fool's gold; in the past, they were worth much more than gold to his contemporaries. The seer stones were allegedly implanted into the framework of large spectacles, and thus, allowed Smith to wear them rather than holding them (for convenience, of course). Some witnesses say that Smith didn't consistently wear the stones, but that he did indeed put them into a hat; not for the laughs, but in order to block out the natural lighting from the outside to better see the translation. The stones, according to Smith, allowed him to completely translate the Book of Mormon into English without ever needing to whip out his free internet trial of *Rosetta Stone*.

At one point, Harris' wife, Lucy, had come to Smith's residence demanding to see the plates. By this time, the entire village was either concerned, annoyed, or fixated on Smith's entire story, as would any pre-modern human being in an age of respective ignorance, but Smith explained to her that since he didn't need the plates for the translation, as his seer stones gave him the information necessary, he buried them deep in the woods. Since Lucy was Martin's wife, and as a married male knows today, you must please the wife in order to maintain both sanity and manhood alike, Martin followed Smith's tracks throughout the wooded area to the place that Smith had supposedly gone to see the plates. In the end, it was a wild goose chase; no plates were ever found.

After the translations were complete, it was officially published for the public at large in 1830. As with all religious formation, there was an overwhelming amount of opposition and criticism toward Smith. This was the first, and one of the last, times that a man had claimed to be a direct prophet of God in quite some time; people do not take prophetic claims without a whim of scrutiny. By this point, Smith had a flock of followers who he led around the Midwest, first in Ohio (where Smith and Oliver Cowdery, cohort in all things LDS, were beaten unconscious and then tarred and feathered), then in Missouri (where they were persecuted, bullied, and then massacred), and eventually settling in Nauvoo, Illinois; Nauvoo is a settlement that Smith actually founded himself, in a wooded, swampy landscape along the Mississippi River.

In Nauvoo, Smith had found a somewhat tolerant home front for the growing Mormon congregation. Missouri was being criticized for the ways in which they handled the growing Mormon congregation, and Illinois played beautiful politics by opening their doors wide for Mormon settlement. After going through all of the official documentation, as well as submitting permission to be an independent territory in the United States (so as they could use militia as protection), Smith had finally created a settlement unto his own. However, this did not last long, and after he had found himself in hot water within the political infrastructure of Illinois, i.e. proposing to the wives of military generals and important political figures. Originally members of the Mormon community, these individuals were excommunicated by Smith in a paranoid frenzy, and then established a competing church.

The dissidents published a newspaper intentionally to push the information that Smith was not only a polygamist, but a man who worshipped multiple God's and was attempting to create a massive theocratic monarchy by which he was king. Smith, fearing that the newspaper would bring hellfire upon the Mormons in Nauvoo, ordered the newspaper to be destroyed. Not understanding the potential consequences of his actions in silencing dissidence, Smith inadvertently incited a mob riot against him. This alone was enough for the authorities at the time to bring Smith down and lock him into a jail cell with his brother Hyrum.

Whilst in jail, a group of individuals masked by black paint on their faces entered the jail cell. In heroic fashion, Hyrum was attempting to hold the jail cell door closed so as to protect his brother Joseph. He was killed by a gunshot to the face instantaneously, leaving the mob to deal with Smith alone. Knowing his impending fate, Smith sprang forth from his position, firing a pistol toward the mob that had been smuggled into his prison cell. He was shot multiple times attempting to flee, falling out of the window and dying after he hit the ground beneath him. There were five men that were tried for the murder of Joseph Smith, Jr. Of the five men, all of them were acquitted. Smith was buried in Nauvoo, but his religion and ideologies remained well into the next two centuries. His impact on the religious settings internationally have been profound, but it is vital to understand not only *why* this is the case, but how he went about constructing potentially the greatest con of all time.

If it pleases the reader, as it should, I would like to rewind back to some of the information presented about the story of Smith. To begin with, the entire story of finding, dictating, transcribing, and publishing the Book of Mormon is impeccably suspicious. For one, Smith was only twenty-four at the time that these great visions came to be. Not only that, but they came out of the sheer blue; divine intervention, I think not. There are two prominent theories that do not relate to anything remotely religious, and I believe they should be not only presented but understood, as they serve to provide us with an understanding of how religious formation comes about.

The first theory is one that is disputed by both believers and non-believers alike. It has generally been discarded by the knowing-public up until this point, but I believe that it is very much akin to something a religious figure would do today; for that reason alone, I will discuss it. It was rumored long ago that one Solomon Spalding was writing a fiction novel entitled *Manuscript Found* about an ancient group of North American "mound-builders". Before we drift into a massive conspiracy theory, I will be the first to assert that the tale is somewhat farfetched, but not too distant from a possible truth. Plagiarism has been well known in all forms of mythological revelation, and all religions essentially stem from folklore piggybacking. However, members of the Spalding family actually signed affidavits claiming that parts of the Book of Mormon were identical to that of Spalding's manuscript.

A fully published version of his manuscript was done so posthumously, and the theory has since been considered debunked. What leaves some mystery behind is how a whole family of individuals can corroborate, under sworn testimony (whatever that meant at the time), on something so uncannily familiar to them. Furthermore, Spalding was known to have various editions of the manuscript, in variously edited forms and formats, lying about. Is it possible that Smith could have easily gotten ahold of one of these unfinished copies and, in a rush of excitement, plagiarized parts of the manuscript? He did, however, come off of the rails of history and into that of fiction with his "early settlers", so it is not so implausible to completely discount the theory of plagiarism.

The other theory is that Smith had simply applied his cultural heritage, that being what was around his village or town at the time, to the ideologies found in the Book of Mormon. Christianity was vastly prevalent in the Midwest, and during his youth, Smith had been greatly influenced by it. The particular region Smith grew up in was considered a hotbed of religious fundamentalism and activity. Another interesting notation about Smith's upbringing is the use of religious folk magic in his family, which is well documented by Mormon and secular scholars alike. The definition of religious folk magic is "anything that is outside of the customary norms of the religion, whereby the boundaries between orthodox and unorthodox are blurred". For instance, many Christians during Christmas celebrate in pagan fashion, such as feasting before the winter solstice, which is strictly outside orthodox Christian ritual. So Smith may not have been practicing cannibalism under the full moon, but the simple fact that he was identifying himself with unorthodox religious practices shows his inclination to promote religious variation, thus giving us a broader understanding of why he was so inclined to create a religion unto himself.

This point brings us to our next discussion. Why did Joseph Smith so deeply fear letting those curious to see the golden plates?

According to LDS historians, it was due to the set of commandments given by Moroni to Smith. They went as followed, taken from the writings of Smith himself:

"Again, he told me, that when I got those plates of which he had spoken—for the time that they should be obtained was not yet fulfilled—I should not show them to any person; neither the breastplate with the Urim and Thummim; only to those to whom I should be commanded to show them; if I did I should be destroyed. While he was conversing with me about the plates, the vision was opened to my mind that I could see the place where the plates were deposited, and that so clearly and distinctly that I knew the place again when I visited it."

So, in essence, Smith created an elaborate proposition from the angel Moroni that fabricated a loophole for those who became interested in knowing about the plates. By the end of Smith's lifespan, he had indeed shown these things to those he deemed worthy. Eleven men were given the opportunity to spectate upon the stones, the plates, and the final manuscript. They even went as far as signing testimonials saying that they had done just that. The Book of Mormon describes the witnessing as having been done with "spiritual eyes", rather than just plain sight. This fact is interesting, as the conflict between Smith having a physical object in his hands would imply that they could actually see, touch, smell, and taste, if one were inclined to do so, the plates of Nephi. Furthermore, all of the witnesses (excluding the aforementioned Martin Harris) were all related to either Joseph Smith or his partner, David Whitmer. In fact, there is a common story about the Book of Mormon called "The Three Witnesses", whereby Oliver Cowdery, Harris, and Whitmer were directly shown the plates by God himself in conjunction with the other eight witnesses. As we know of today, no objective party was ever given the opportunity.

Positing a theory about Smith's paranoia is very easy to do. First and foremost, Smith was already known around his community as deceitful, so pushing a new religion in that territory besmirched his position from the beginning. The fear of persecution be it that the community discovered he had lied was also a dire problem that was under constant watch by Smith. This is why he persisted that the translation after losing the original manuscript wasn't going to have the exact same wording, as if adversaries had gotten ahold of the document, Smith could have been easily denounced as fraudulent when his stories did not corroborate one another's details. His paranoia is further pronounced when we look at Moroni's commandment of not using the plates for monetary gain (as they were both made of solid gold and revelatory). As we have seen in the past, psychologically, when an individual promotes contraception, the first thought that enters our mind is sexuality. Much is the same with Smith, whereby when we read that he was told not to use the plates, and subsequent religion, for monetary gain, he true intentions were to get rich, and do so quickly. This theory also corresponds with the fact that Smith's family was incredibly impoverished at the time he had written the Book of Mormon.

As a confidence man, Joseph Smith had spent his time procuring one of the greatest frauds of the 19th century. In an age where America had no stable economy, governmental system, or identifiable culture, Smith's ideas were beyond convenient to implant in the minds of his people. It was easy for him, for example, to attempt to create a story of America's origins, as we had no knowledge of the Norse settlements hundreds of years before, nor did we have any notion of where exactly Native American Indian populations had migrated from; for all we knew, their culture had evolved from the victorious Lamanites.

But to condemn Smith for his actions is past-due in terms of the rest of the religious leaders. If anything, Smith was only the tip of the iceberg. As you follow that iceberg down, all the way to the tales in the Old Testament roughly 2,500 years before, you will see that mixed in with the cultural heritage of the Jewish peoples was an elaborate attempt to explain the meaning of human existence. Smith wasn't the first individual to abuse the powers of knowledge (or for that matter, fabricated knowledge) in order to obtain power. It has been a long process, from the New Testament stories of Jesus Christ, to the tales found in the Qur'an involving the infamous Mohammed, Smith was just another brick in the wall. This is not to detract from his significance, however. He has created the fasted growing religion in the Western world, and from his influence, political leaders, cornerstone figures of the global economy, and other powerful, important individuals have immerged. This is the power of religion, and that should not be ignored.

What we can learn from studying the story of Joseph Smith is that as long as there is religious tolerance, there will be religious reformation. Ideas that have been societally extinct for the past centuries, decades, or even days are found amongst the pages of religious "tradition". Tradition is something to be feared, as it represents the absence of change. Without societal change, we cannot have societal progress. Without a doubt, there will be another Joseph Smith in the woodworks. He will abuse the trust and confidence of those around him using familiar, comfortable literary archetypes and formulas, and furthermore, will gain monetary and personal wealth, power, and infinitely more frighteningly, influence. The modernized world can deal with influence, but through the backdoor comes the archaic, oppressive religious folkways and mores that will dominate a society in the long-run; in the end, tolerating intolerance will bring us to a deficit, and leave those who follow religious authority moral bankruptcy.

# CHAPTER 12
## *Jehovah's Witnesses*

*"Is God willing to prevent evil, but not able? Then he is not omnipotent.*
*Is he able, but not willing? Then he is malevolent.*
*Is he both able and willing? Then whence cometh evil?*
*Is he neither able nor willing? Then why call him God?"*

*Epicurus*

I graduated high school with a C-minus average. Typically, that isn't something anyone wants to outwardly admit, but because it is entirely relevant to the subsequent text, I have shared it. I wasn't entirely sure of where I wanted to go with my future. I wasn't particularly book smart (irony aside), and my parents didn't have enough money to invest in sending me to a university or college; I probably, at the time, would have failed out anyway. I knew, out of all things, that I needed to find an occupation of the lower-educational variety. Skimming through newspapers, I consistently applied for positions which fell into such a domain. These were the sort of jobs that had few actual requirements: read at—or up to—an eighth grade level, be moderately good at taking orders and interpreting intercom phrases (such as "clean up on aisle 7" or "I would like fries with that"). Even though I took and participated in these positions, I knew I wanted and needed something with more substance. On the bus home from the inner city every day, I would steal a newspaper from wherever I was working at a given time and search for such professional enlightenment.

One in particular caught my attention. Although the specific details of the classified advertising are now blurry, it went something like: "big company looking to expand team; no experience necessary; guaranteed pay minimum 2000 a month." That was the line; the hook was that applicants could be involved in "set-up and display," which was entirely suitable for a man of minimal scholastic credentials. I had assumed that the job would appertain to marketing the products in a window display; in anxiety, I dreamt of the all the permutations that evening. I sent in my resume, and to my complete surprise, they called me for an interview that next day. This should have been the initial and final warning sign.

The day of the interview I put on a suit too small for comfort. I felt like Bruce Banner walking through those warehouse doors, on the verge of exploding in a bout of green fury if I were to have brought my arms just inches closer to one another. My pants were so tight that my genitalia emitted screams from behind a metal zippered curtain of despair. I understood at that moment what it felt like to hold the high expectations of a corset a hundred years before; except mine was fitted to my entire 93 pound frame. In this most uncomfortable moment, I greeted the interviewer. Although all of the circumstances were against me, amidst the sea of people waiting to be interviewed, I felt that the interview had gone well. I found out that night that it had indeed.

That evening they had called to tell me that I got the job. My parents were exceptionally proud of their typically lackluster son, and the hope of a blossoming career in "set-up and display" was well underway. If only I had a piece of paper with the confirmation on it. It would wind up right on the blank white fridge door that held all the other major accomplishments in my life. For that previous six months, I had been doing mediocre, mindless tasks in order to make money that was just *barely* enough to subsist on. Now that I was in the field of "Set Up and Display," I had no more worries.

On my first day of work, I rode the bus from where we lived into the city. It took approximately seventy-five minutes to get from point *A* to *B*. That day, I showed up ninety minutes early, as you could never be *too* early for your first day of work. The address was located at a large warehouse, and no one else was around. So I loitered around the block until I was certain that there was life entering the building. When I looked about the parking lot, en route to the entranceway, I noticed a surplus of lush, extravagant vehicles. The anticipation at the prospects of a rich future commenced as I imagined the amount of money people made in "set-up and display"; this was a very exciting moment for me.

A gentle and kind woman greeted us in the hallway, pointing to the location of our orientation. All of the newer individuals being orientated on the job rallied like cattle to the open room, and I followed suit. There were approximately 150 other people at the orientation, consisting of young, old, white, black, man, and woman. This amount of diversity impressed me, and it left a remarkable imprint on the ways in which the company worked right off the bat. The anticipation climbed ever steeper.

As we sat on the stools and collected ourselves, an attractive, charismatic individual came out to a small podium centered and raised above the congregation of potential employees. He gave a speech that, to this day, I have never forgotten. His grammar and diction were superb. The words he said flowed out of his mouth like a gentle stream, only to open into a delta of candid ears and watchful eyes. He said things like:

> "…. This company was founded on finding good people who others have thrown away… if you want more than your parents ever had… the system is simple… guaranteed future… you can drive a Porsche for fun and a BMW for a grocery getter…"

I had thought, by this point, I had found what I had been searching for. I had finally found a place of belonging; it made me feel comfortable and hopeful for what was to come. There was a point in his speech where I knew precisely how to approach the job of "set-up and display," and then, at that exact moment, realized he still hadn't given me any further details. This was when he introduced what we would be marketing and selling door to door:

### Vacuum Cleaners

Of course, in his eyes, this vacuum cleaner was, to the core of his being, the greatest vacuum cleaner ever manufactured for the general public, and all other vacuums paled in comparison. He went into great detail about its ability to inhale all that it found before it; he even accentuated all of the bonus attachments that came along, just to get into the nooks and crannies that, perhaps, were impossible to reach with a different cleaner. The rant continued on, explaining all of the benefits that it could potentially provide for the user, as well as those around said user.

Suddenly, three-quarters of the room stood up and left. You could cut the tension, embarrassment, and panic from the quarter left behind with a dull knife. But this leader, one of charisma and understanding, stood before those exiting with a complete lack of vindictiveness. He said reassuring things to the group before him, who were moments before laughing at his sales pitch. And then I realized that I should have been amongst those who left. But something about this particular man, company, and organization left me feeling as if I truly *belonged* to something, even though it was related to something as mundane as vacuum cleaners.

For a while, my position in the company was hugely progressive. I sold eight vacuums in my first month, surpassing my goal of two the first month. However, after the first month, I ran out of available, wealthy family members. So I figured I would tell my team leader, the one who rallied the final quarter together, that I could no longer accomplish the tasks my occupation required. He looked at me intently, his eyes full of purpose and poise. He began his argument as such:

> "Well, I am sorry to hear that you haven't quite acclimated yourself to our system. But let me ask you this. How were you to ever sell one of our vacuum cleaners if you had never owned one yourself? How could you possibly promote something you had no previous ownership of? In my business, we would call such an individual fraudulent; we know from experience that the customer can see that you are a fraud the second you attempt to sell them something you have never *experienced* holistically."

And on that note, not only did I quit my job with the company a few weeks later, but I was the owner of a squeaky clean, high-performing, two thousand dollar vacuum cleaner to put right next to my perfectly fine working, practical, economical vacuum in the closet.

The reason I introduced the chapter with this story is simple. The man was a natural leader, as I have asserted before. He was able to assemble a group of individuals and promote to them what they would inevitably promote to others. But what is more striking is that for him, his motivations were based on *numbers*; it was the quantity, rather than the quality, that he accounted for. He was a businessman, and he knew his target market, his margins of both profit and loss, and furthermore, how he would deal with members of his company on a macro-scale. With me alone, like so many others before me and after me, in the beginning there are promises of wealth, heaven on earth, cars, parties, everything an uneducated and impressionable person wants. To his credit, through me, he had sold nine vacuums and when he was done with me, when I had served his purpose, I did not matter anymore. When I didn't want to go door to door anymore, and when I didn't want to attend another sales training, I was spit out; never to be talked to again. Certainly his boss was happy with him, as he made a 2,000 dollar investment and returned $18,000 on it in just four weeks. It took me quite some time to realize that he operated on the synonymous motives of religious authority.

Religious leaders, and especially the Jehovah's Witness and the Watch Tower Society, are superlative in their uses of persuasion. For them, the larger the organization, as well as the more dedicated, the easier *their* jobs become. The Jehovah's Witnesses are essentially a prime example of excellent marketing. The more individuals they confront at their homes, or on the streets, perhaps even in their own place of worship, statistically the higher number of converts will be collected. There is bound to be someone who has recently lost someone they loved; whose wife was just diagnosed with a fatal variation of cancer; who is confused about their sexual identity or feels guilty for a particular fetish; who thinks they are truly possessed by a demon or devil. The Jehovah's Witnesses, with a masterful precision, find individuals in these vulnerable positions and make the most of their emotional resources. Like the businessman, they will go for the cheapest, most convenient way to attain a profit.

Although I am not a Jehovah's Witness, I was never afraid to allow them inside of my own home when they came to my door. In fact, I made it a *mission*, so to speak, to stop everything I was occupied with at that given moment in order to socialize and learn about their culture; it almost gives me butterflies in the pit of my stomach. However, this mode of absorption is rarely practiced by other people. Not surprisingly, many Christians will avoid their not-so-distant cousins when they come around. They, of course, have already found the truth; an atheist is one who has found all the answers they need through science and humanity.

The Jehovah's Witnesses are very notable for a slew of reasons. For starters, they comprise one of the newer cults to be accepted into the mainstream, albeit still considered exceptional to the traditional veins of Christian philosophy. They are a relatively new phenomenon, surfacing from research done by Charles Taze Russell, an American minister. Russell's work began in 1870 on the Bible, and was intended to question outdated beliefs propagated by Christian pastors of the time, i.e. hellfire, the "Holy Trinity," inherent immortality of the soul, so forth. The primary inquisition centered itself around whether or not the scriptures of the Bible actually *supported* these elements, rather than using them as points of reference or metaphors.

What eventually culminated were several documents that Russell deemed a more accurate account of the events of scripture, even going as far as to revise the chronology of the Bible and attempt to approximate the "end-times." By 1879, Russell established based on the text what was then known as "Zion's Watch Tower and Herald of Christ's Presence." These eventually became monthly publications, a practice the Jehovah's Witnesses still maintain, now in the form of "Watchtower" magazine, as the former was a mouthful; it was also probably much more difficult to market, but that comes much later.

In 1881, based around his studies and previous organizations and writings, Russell formed the "Zion's Watch Tower and Tract Society." Although he was not president (those duties were relegated to William Henry Conley, a native industrialist and philanthropist from Pittsburgh), he served as its "secretary treasurer," providing the driving force behind his mechanical sprawl of literature and religious proliferation. It was from this organization that his writings became fully-fleshed out publications, circulating around the United States like wildfire. As these began to become more popular, he published weekly sermons in newspapers; by the end of this, he had his sermons in roughly 4,000 syndicated newspapers internationally. In fact in 1910 *Overland Monthly*, a secular journal located in California, noted that he was the most widely independently distributed writer in the English language in the United States, as well as being third in the most circulated works on earth; he was beat out by the Bible itself, as well as the Chinese almanac[32].

Today, utilizing Russell's monumental texts, deemed "Studies of the Scriptures," a group of men now orchestrate all doctrinal output of the Jehovah's Witnesses. These individuals, synonymous to a common African tribe, dictate precisely what is to be preached within the religion. That means that their interpretation of events, history, and religious theory are entirely dependent on how they felt when they woke up. As far as they are concerned, much like the Catholic Pope, they are infallible. It is important to note that women are not allowed to be in positions of authority, as they are looked upon as subordinate to men; this is probably due to organizational skills, and their keen ability to ensure dates and facts are reconciled with reality.

Russell "discovered" a number of things, most of which contradict core tenets of mainstream Christianity. We will concern ourselves with the primary instances, and branch out from there. To begin, it is essential to know that Jehovah's Witnesses separate from their religious cousins when it comes to acknowledging the "Holy Trinity." They recognize God as a single being, rather than Jesus Christ (the son), the Holy Spirit, and God himself (the father). This is important. Russell believed that, although divine, Christ was only divine at the point of sacrificing himself. He also notes that the Holy Spirit is not an individual person but a manifestation of the "power of God."

The second distinguishing aspect is the "order of events," so to speak, from which all of mankind unfolded. At the first instance of life, we have God, which is referred to as Jehovah; this is allegedly the Hebrew name for "God." He creates two angels: Michael and Lucifer. Since we already know how the latter winds up, we will cut to the story of Michael. In Witness theology, they believe that Michael is actually Jesus Christ in a pre-human (and inevitably post-human) form. Because of Adam and Eve, who were seduced by Lucifer, Michael is recreated by Jehovah as Jesus, in order to pursue the "torture stake" (not cross), sacrificing himself for all humanity. Russell had imagined that these events, including the actual creation of the Earth, took place over a period of 42,000 years. I suppose

---

[32] Overland Monthly, January 1910 p. 130

credit is due, as he was, in the very least, closer than his terribly off-the-mark Christian ancestors.

Russell believed that Christ was supposed to have risen by 1914, and simultaneously, Satan as well. Coincidentally, this was near the time frame of World War I, and many modern Jehovah's Witnesses grant this event as the "coming of Christ." They are said to have remained here, and we can assume that they are responsible in some form for all of the major wars and catastrophes since then. Beforehand, however, there is a bit of a grey area as to whom the blame falls upon; perhaps exclusively God.

In their theology, Heaven is still a religious construct and motivational mechanism. However, unlike the common Christian belief, it is reserved for only 144,000 Witnesses. There are no approximations as to how many places are left; I will assume at the Pearly Gates that they draw straws. Therefore, Heaven is used to maintain an air of civility and obedience, and Jehovah's Witnesses must abide by Jehovah's dictation but to get into their Heaven, to take one of the 144,000 places, you have to be one of their popes; they are the only ones who certainly get to Heaven and hang out with God. For the rest of the congregation, once a Jehovah's Witness dies, they succumb to permanent darkness. In this sense, atheists and Witnesses philosophically coincide. The comparison ends, however, when they are "resurrected" in Heaven on Earth. For the ones who don't get to go to Heaven, God will recreate the Garden of Eden on Earth and there they shall live, hopefully this time without any apple trees and snakes, and the Jehovah's Witnesses will get to play in a massive park for the rest of eternity.

In order to maintain their religious fervor, they attend, on average, five meetings a week. At this point, similarly to Christianity, they are taught from the texts of the Watchtower publications. For newly acquired members, they must study these documents for a minimum of six months before elders will consider them viable and dedicated enough to be baptized. Before this can happen, the elders give them a "pop-quiz." If they pass said quiz, they are granted admission and become prophets. We can assume that this is part of a grander scheme, as the less dedicated members will be weeded out, and thus, far fewer resources are wasted upon them.

Once members of the congregation, they are required to maintain an air of modesty; this ranges from their actions as members of society as well as to their dress, habits, diet, relationships, language, and whatever else you could imagine comprising your daily activities. They cannot participate in government elections, join any military organization (nor salute or promote anything related), or do yoga even if they do have a bad back , and they must avoid holidays like the plague. They are each required to submit a schedule of "public canvassing," in order to case neighborhoods and spread Witness propaganda and literature.

The dastardly aspect of this implied agreement is very illuminating of the Jehovah's Witness' true nature. If a member of the congregation breaks any of the above regulations, they risk excommunication from the church (called "disfellowshipping"). Not only is this dangerous to the party involved, but it is also precarious for the members of their family. If the daughter of a Jehovah's Witness enters a room with her mother in it and she has been disfellowshipped, the mother will not even acknowledge her existence. As soon as an excommunication commences, all members of the family being banished are treated as social lepers. This is condoned by the Witness' elite. Not unlike their Anglican and Catholic cousins, the Jehovah's Witnesses have also had their share of sex scandals, but the difference is that only very few of the Jehovah's Witness cases come to light because of the policy and threat of disfellowshipping. All of the children who were abused by members of their church from Denmark to Delaware and have come out with their stories have all been disfellowshipped. Their parents will not talk to them nor will any person of their family and their lifetime friends, as they have hurt their church with their truths. The Jehovah's Witnesses through these actions are not punishing the child abusers, but rather punishing the abused. They choose to condone child rape rather than do anything to hurt the Watch Tower Society. All over the world the Jehovah's Witnesses, who may not so much like the government but certainly love its laws are spending millions of dollars, euros, and kroners, to defend child molesters and to suppress newspapers with lawsuits and threats as reported by the victims of the molesters and reported by the ICSA[33] in 2007 that the Watch Tower would "sue them into poverty."

To add to the severity of the Witnesses' dogmatic religious principles, they also extend exile to anyone who belongs to another

---

[33] ICSA Newsletter, Vol. 6, No. 2, 2007

religion; although this is quite common among religious leaders, the Jehovah's Witnesses take it to another extreme. They believe, for instance, that Christianity is "apostate," overflowing with pastors who are representative antichrists. These pastors are responsible for operating churches run by Satan himself. And as the topping on the Witnesses' layer cake, they also find the support of "earthly governance," i.e., the democratic system of the United States or in Europe, as rather objectionable in the eyes of the Lord. Perhaps they would prefer anarchy? I suppose that would be counterintuitive to their hierarchical structural integrity.

The main contention that modern Christian theologians have with Jehovah's Witnesses' practice is that their (very recent) religious text comes from a strange variety of Hebrew, Greek, and Aramaic. Of course, the Holy Bible falls into this category as well. The primary distinction is that, when published, the individuals responsible for translation had very little to do with the respective languages. Let us begin by introducing a few primary players in the game of Russell's vision:

> **Frederick Franz**: Some biblical translators do leave Franz alone as to his translation abilities, as he was the only individual who had a classical training in *some* amount of the language used in the Witness texts. His training came from his liberal arts degree, acquired at the University of Cincinnati. The actual training in translation came from a mere twenty-one hours of classical Greek, minor Latin, and a complete *two hour* survey course in Biblical Greek during his senior year. He was self-taught in Spanish, biblical Hebrew, and Aramaic; yet, when put on the spot he doesn't really perform as one might expect.

In an attempt to set the record straight, the court of law in Edinburgh, Scotland in 1954 administered a basic test (which Franz failed) in order to assess his grasp on the Hebrew language. They found, naturally, that Franz had no actual skills in terms of reading, writing, or speaking the Hebrew language[34]:

---

[34] Transcript 1954, Edinburgh Scotland

| Cross: | *"You, yourself, read and speak Hebrew, do you?"* |
|---|---|
| Franz: | *"I do not speak Hebrew."* |
| Cross: | *"You do not?"* |
| Franz: | *"No."* |
| Cross: | *"Can you, yourself, translate that INTO HEBREW?"* |
| Franz: | *"Which?"* |
| Cross: | *"That fourth verse of the Second Chapter of Genesis?"* |
| Franz: | *"You mean here?"* |
| Cross: | *"Yes."* |
| Franz: | *"No. I WON'T ATTEMPT TO DO THAT."* |

As we know, to tell a lie is okay, but to tell a lie under oath means Franz would be going to Hell as he has sinned against god. There is no commandment that says " Thou shalt not falsely translate the bible for the sole purpose of promoting your church's agenda!" Yet, it does say thou shalt not bear false witness, which as we know specifically means in court It makes one wonder why he would not attempt to translate Genesis and admit that he didn't speak Hebrew, doesn't it?

**George Gangas**: One of the translators who had virtually *zero* training in the translation and understanding of historical language. He was a Turkish national who had a rudimentary grasp of *modern* Greek, which happened to be the language he was translating the publications into.

**Milton Henschel, Karl Klein, and Nathan Knorr**: *Zero* Biblical language experience.

**Albert Schroeder**: The last of the translators for the publications. He had no background in Biblical language; he was actually a mechanical engineer who dropped out by his third year.

Yet even though it is near impossible for a translation to do justice to an original text, and anyone who speaks more than one language knows when something is written in a native language and then translated to another, something is always lost in the translation; something is always missing and I find it is highly hypocritical that Christian theologians point to the Jehovah's Witnesses' texts as falsified based exclusively on the incompetence of their translators. It is well-documented that the original language of the Bible (written far behind even the authors of the Old Testament) was a broken, archaic language that modern linguists are still attempting to wrap their minds around. So much like the game "Telephone," played by kindergarteners around the globe, a clear phrase can wind up a muddy paragraph in an instant.

One of the primary mistranslations, for which not only the Witnesses are characteristically guilty of, appertain to the misappropriation of the title for God. In all technical senses of the word, God and all of his misnomers and aliases can be traced back to one name found in Old Testament scripture: *YHWH*. This word is not an acronym, but consists solely of consonants, thus making the pronunciation of the name increasingly difficult for non-Hebrew speakers. Therefore, they personally refer to God as *Adonai*; we will assume it comes from their superstition of speaking falsely the Lord thy God's name in vain, or however that goes. Christians and especially the Jehovah's Witnesses eventually utilized the vowel sounds of *Adonai* and applied them to *YHWH*. They came up with *Yahowah*. This, because of Western culture, inevitably became *Yahweh*, which is commonly how we spell and pronounce the initial name of God. As a human contrivance, Russell and his followers developed it to *Jehovah*, which albeit far off the map, rolls off the tongue far easier.

Why must we dwell on such miniscule details, you may ask? Well it is as simple as this. Let's say that, because my name is Lance and I live in Germany, individuals began to pronounce my name as *Lanze*, which they often do. Not only is this tremendously frustrating to be a part of, but it is also entirely *false*. The implied meaning of my name as *Lance* is far and away different than, linguistically, the meaning for *Lanze*. Inevitably, my name will become something like *Lansche*, which will mean, once again, something entirely different. We can go as far as blaming the evolutionary nature of language, but we must consider the implications. As translations and pronunciations evolve from one variation to another, so do meanings and purposes. This is chaos theory at its most fundamental, and poses potentially dangerous repercussions, as we have seen amongst the feuding religions and their wars. Jehovah's Witnesses maintain that Jehovah is the correct name for God, and He must be referred to as such, and not calling him Jehovah is a major sin. Yet just like the school yard bully who used to call me Lance Garbagetruck to drive me insane, the minute you start playing with the name of Jehovah or YHWH, if you are not pronouncing the name of a person correctly it very much frustrates the owner of said name. Now do that over and over again hundreds of times a week, and I am pretty certain if it was me, I would be thinking you were just calling me Lance Garbagetruck and I would seriously think you are taking my name in vain.

To pronounce the word YHWH in Hebrew you need to make a sound like you are trying to spit up a fur ball lodged in your throat. Now I am just making assumptions, but I am pretty sure most Jehovah's Witnesses cannot say the name correctly, and remember, if you say *His* name wrong, according to the Watch tower writings, then you are not waking up in paradise.

One of things every atheist, or really any person of belief as well should do when confronted by a Jehovah's Witness is to ask that Witness' name at the beginning during the introductions and then pronounce his or her name wrong through the entire conversation. Now, let's say their name is James. Call him Jameez, Jamesses, Ja-Mez and Jammies, and watch as they get upset as to you always saying their name wrong after they bring up the Scriptures, and the "if you found a watch" argument, and just ask them why they have to call god "Jehovah" and then use my argument.

If the world is going to end in the Jehovah's Witnesses' lifetime, wouldn't it make sense to prepare for it? With that statement I mean that if the doctor gave me just a few years to live, I probably would do everything for the moment and not look at long term investments as a way to enjoy my life in the years ahead. Yet the leadership at the watch tower seems to think that although they preach a short term investment, they actually bank on a long one.

It is well known that Jehovah's Witnesses, among their excellent marketing practices to benefit the size of the congregation, are also excellent financiers in other aspects of the economy. For example, Witness organizations are marked on the financial ledgers of some of the most historical and lavish properties in the world. One of these is *Hotel Bossert*, once called the "Waldorf-Astoria" of Brooklyn. In 1988, this property was purchased by none other than the Watchtower chapter in New York; it is arguably one of the more recognized purchases of the Witnesses. They began leasing space out in 1983, and with their gross amount of revenues from their religious business, they decided to outright buy it. The purpose for this:

provide living quarters for free for their members. If you were not a Jehovah's Witness, then you had to pay the applicable fees. By 2010, they had renovated it back for its original use as a hotel.

This purchase was not necessarily *malevolent*. The Witnesses purchased the property legally; they went through the appropriate governmental veins in order to obtain and renovate it. Yet there is something about this that leaves a terrible taste on the palate. According to local real estate agents and brokers, the Witnesses own a collective 1 *billion* dollars in parking lots, hotels, and various office structures just in the Brooklyn Heights and Dumbo areas of New York. It begs the question: *why?* Parking lots, hotels, and office structures are not short term investments. These are long term, solid investments; if you as an investor wanted to maximize your short term gains, say in the belief that the world was going to end in your life time, then hedge funds, investing in IPO's, anything with a short term gain would make sense. Yet, if you knew the world wasn't going to end then the best investment would be in things like property, parking lots and office buildings, wouldn't it? Anything else would be classified as a Ponzi scheme. Isn't it funny that when Bernard Maddoff or Allen Stanford ran their Ponzi schemes and swindled thousands of people out of billions of dollars, promising a return they could never give, we looked upon them as a cancer on society, but when the Jehovah's Witnesses do it, we tolerate them? Why? Because they believe in god.

As a religious organization, financial endeavors generally apply to your own institution in relation to your congregation. They would invest in, say, a new church or place of worship that provides greater comfort, or higher and higher ceilings; perhaps (as we know God is a fan of) gold-laced toilet seats. And then we must consider where they get all their revenue.

It is well-known that most religious institutions use some variation of the *collection plate*; whether or not this is actually a plate. The religious leaders coax the members of the congregation to give their well-earned money to the church, so as they cannot further promote the word of God. Although you would be hard pressed to find it in Watch Tower Literature, the Jehovah's Witnesses admit that most people give by a *percentage* of their income. The accepted standard is now 10% (which, as they say is less then what is expecting for tipping a waiter), presumably annually or collectively over a given year. So not only do we have to contend with the fact that churches are doing this in an entirely unethical manner, but also that the congregation is *allowing* it.

Of course, not all of their revenue could come from collection plates. There are simply not enough members (or high enough percentiles of wealth) to buy extravagant historical properties on a regular basis. The Jehovah's Witnesses are exceptionally good at convincing both long-term members and new converts to give up their properties in light of all that is holy. The Witnesses then go right around and sell these properties, primarily if they serve no further purpose to them. They are often documented entering an individual's life, such as an elderly family, and essentially waiting for them to pass away. More often than not, by the end of it all, that family will have willed their estate to the Witnesses.

The question of *why* will be answered now. First, let's address one of the motivating factors for a religious member of the Jehovah's Witnesses. Since Hell does not exist on the Witness books (poor strategy by the way), another mechanism to instill fear into their members hearts naturally had to convene. This is Armageddon, stolen from the mythologies of past Christians and propagated yet again. Not only do the Witnesses have to practically compete in a no-holds barred moral adrenaline rush, but they also have to contend with the idea that even if they aren't a member of the 144,000 that get to frolic in the clouds and cascade through heavenly mountains, they will die long before their time when Jesus comes back and will be waiting for him to wake them up.

Given this information, why is the *long-term* even in consideration? Why invest in all of the stocks and bonds, properties, and real estate in so many regions and countries? The entire world is going to end, and yet there is still room for this? The answer is simple, and answers every aspect of the Witness theology; their motivation; their obsession. The Witness elite don't actually *believe* any of it at all. They are now a corporate, worldwide entity. They found a market, and they capitalized it vehemently. They created a new mythology for those who they knew would buy into it, and now sell volumes of their own beliefs to their members at full retail price. The Jehovah's Witnesses were never interested in saving the souls of the desolate.

The arguments against the Jehovah's Witnesses are many, but when they do ring my door, and I do invite them in, I enjoy asking talking to them and asking what would happen if I joined the religion and my wife did too, but then she left. When you ask them if there is anyone in their lives that they don't speak with anymore because of non-belief, maybe a grandchild that they will never hold, maybe a mother who they will never see again, and you ask them what if they are wrong? Or "don't you actually miss them? Because I would not be able to live without my kids around me." Or why they are not allowed to question anything that their church says and why they are not allowed to have an opinion about anything, or "You must just do what the Watch Tower says; if they said tomorrow to drink this Kool-Aid, then you would have to do it, wouldn't you?" They will then, and only then, understand that they are actually slaves living in a totalitarian dictatorship worse than the one that exists in modern day North Korea.

# CHAPTER 13
## *Islam*

*Only Sheep need a shepherd!*

*— Anonymous*

I will begin this chapter by explaining its broader purpose as an exclusive chapter. Although we have discussed many religions, philosophies, theories, and pseudo-scientific principles throughout our logical discourse, none of them hold a candle to the amount of intensity and controversy, especially since the events of September 11th, 2001, than that of the Islamic faith. Instead of reveling in this controversy, as we can write an entire book on this single faith and its historical atrocities, we will focus rather on its founder, and the consequences of obtaining too much power. It will be a backdrop and a lesson for those who are currently in a position of religious authority, and it is not particular to just the Muslim world.

There are innumerable arguments from a Christian point of view as to why the Muslims got their philosophies wrong. The problem posed by this melting pot of faux-intellectualism is that it is an argument posed from one deist to another. If there is to be any critical analysis of a religion, or in this case a particular religious point of view, then it must be from a naturally objective one. Since this book is dedicated and formulated for those without a religious bias, our qualifications for the latter have been met. However, it goes without saying that Christians have invented some wonderful arguments in opposition to the Islamic universe, but it is hypocritical to take their theories and arguments as we would take our own. We wouldn't take Santa Claus' dislike of the Easter Bunny's practices with a grain of salt, so I won't begin to allow the same leniency for Christians.

Avoiding the argument between two points of faith, we will first focus on a brief history of the troubled Prophet Muhammad. The first interesting fact to note is that the Qur'an describes Muhammad as illiterate, so immediately the validity of his prophecies must be called into question. Because of his illiteracy, Muhammad had to continuously play an ever more intricate game of "Telephone" with his cohorts and scribes. It is alleged that he would remember the prophecies by ear, at which point they were inscribed. Much as the problems with Joseph Smith, we know now that this method produces highly defective material. We can also question whether or not Muhammad was actually alive at the time in which the Qur'an was written, as the oral traditions of the Islamic faith were much stronger than their historically written testimonials.

With this fact aside, his "revelations" occurred in the 6th century CE, which was far after the centuries-old creation of the Old Testament and a few hundred years after the New Testament. The reason this is important is because it is commonly held that the Qur'an is an incredibly old document holding onto very old Islamic traditions; although societal traditions obviously existed, this was the point at which religious Islamic institutionalization was fully realized. Yet it should be known that although Muhammad did know of the spreading of the Christian and now Roman religion throughout the Western world, he would have been informed about the stories contained in their scriptures. He would have gleaned from them the power which the priests, the bishops, and the pope held over common people, and he would have understood the power in the power of belief.

For all intents and purposes, I would now like to express a new theory on the actual Muhammad using literary and historical analysis. To begin with, I will start with the conclusions that I have drawn about Muhammad, and then explain them with all the supporting issues surrounding this enigmatic person. First and foremost, I believe that Muhammad was a corrupt warlord with his own personal agendas, akin to Genghis Khan and more recently, Joseph Kony. Second, he had an adversely sexual fetish with women, which inevitably channels us to the root predicament of the final issue: Muhammad was a jealous and violent man, whose contempt distorted his initial intentions. These three simple issues became much vaster, sinister problems that the Islamic world is still dealing with today, albeit passively and submissively. I believe it is from these things that the controversies surrounding Islam in the 21st century have come to be.

It all began in 613 CE in Mecca, where Muhammad initialized his preaching. It is said that there were three main groups of individuals that became his initial congregation: the mercantile society, those disenfranchised from their tribes, and weak unprotected foreigners. The rest of Mecca found Muhammad to be a joke, and this began a decade-long turmoil with Muhammad and his growing flock. This was the beginning of Muhammad as warlord. The history of his position as a militant leader is hidden amidst his more "prophetic" history, but it remains the same. Utilizing his newly created variation on past Abrahamic religious mythology, and brandishing it with much finesse, he ordered his congregation-turned-militia to storm Mecca.

By this time, Muhammad had already migrated to Medina and begun his military campaign against Mecca. It is said in the Qur'an that Muhammad came to this decision based on a revelation from none other than God himself, who commanded Muhammad to pray toward Mecca rather than Jerusalem; ironically enough, he then led a militant campaign against Mecca, so we can only begin to guess the correlation. He led some three hundred loyal followers to raid Mecca, killing important political figures and their entire army, losing only a handful of his own men. With this win, his validation and status as an official warlord began. What must be understood is that, like so many before him, Muhammad used the power of religion to place him in a position of authority, and took revenge on Mecca for their maltreatment of his congregation and religious philosophy, all the while using God as his scapegoat. Turning yourself into a God is the easiest way to convince individuals to die for you, as they can be reborn in the next life. This principle initiated some of the most horrific things the world has seen at the hands of religion since the advent of the Crusades, but they are now occurring in our sophisticated and socially "advanced" society, and within our lifetime.

As noted, this wasn't the first time a genius military leader used religion as a tool. It has been applied to military strategy for quite some time, and was implemented by Khan in order to achieve cohesion amongst his troops. He fancied himself a messenger of God, and in doing so, was able to explain for his domineering reign of terror: "I am the punishment of God... If you had not committed great sins, God would not have sent a punishment like me upon you." Furthermore, the Mongol nation believed (and some still do) that Khan would (will) rise from the dead, synonymous to the mythology of Christ, and return his people to the status they once attained. In this sense, Muhammad was no different.

The first Islamic military rulings were formulated during the first century after Muhammad had established his Islamic state in Medina. These were in accordance with what he had created in the Qur'an, as well as the recorded traditions of Muhammad in "Hadith." The main objective of these two documents was to solidify the "justness" of war and the infamous injunction of "jihad." Collectively, this is referred to as the correct Islamic manner of wartime military jurisprudence, and must be obeyed at all times. The point in noting this is that these fundamentalist ideas led to a problem now being confronted by the modern, socially developed world, where these defunct principles still struggle ferociously to survive in a new skin.

Muhammad's campaigns didn't end at the front door of Mecca. He used his newly acquired powers to recruit new members of Islam through coercion. As he went on to different nomadic tribal communities, Muhammad offered them allegiance to the increasingly Muslim-controlled Syro-Arabian steppe. If they denied his offer, they were relegated to the areas outside of the latter, and had to remain there. Since their livelihoods remained within the Muslim territory, they were forced to join Islam. This method, although not as violently aggressive, still retained a *Godfather*-esque pastiche, and provided a particularly unfriendly way to join an allegedly peaceful organization.

The tremendous power that Muhammad had acquired had mired his objective as a religious leader. Although he was successful as a military leader, it is hard to imagine looking at him in a godly light after committing to wartime practices. After all, Jesus would never have attempted to dominate a geographic region to unify his congregations and proselytize his Christian philosophy. Muhammad had no inhibitions about this, and rather embraced the status of warlord. So the question then became a matter of "What else would Muhammad sacrifice?" in order to attain an even broader range of followers, and furthermore, more girth for his religion to acclimate on a global scale. This mentality led to some of the most atrocious acts of civil oppression that the modern world is now confronted with. To elaborate, we have to first look at the history of female oppression, as well as the tools that manifested in order to instill it.

As far as we know, women were not always on the lower social rung. Recorded history has provided us with an approximate date of 6,000 years, at which point female oppression began to take form. So Muslims were not the first, nor the last, to have this diluted worldview. At this moment in time, the third world has maintained an air of hostility towards the female race, whether it amounts to forced prostitution (both adult and child), slavery, labor, and the more pertinent topic of discussion, sexual abuse. Many feminists will go on to argue that this behavior is biologically engrained in men; however, to buy into this would be unfair to the true roots of the situation at hand. This oppression has actually changed, and in an incredibly short span of time, proving the feministic theory wrong.

Even in the last few decades, some third world provinces have socially evolved to the status of the first world. Iraq, for instance, has made great advancements from its previous state as one of the penultimate chambers of oppression and violence toward women. The ousting of Saddam Hussein within the last decade has been the key. It is these types of tyrants that have dominated social order, and all of them have been male. Since the topic of this chapter is Muhammad, the focal point will remain on his influence of female oppression and systemic sexual abuse the Islamic nations he fathered so intently.

Before this chapter draws criticism from Muslim and non-Muslim alike, let us outline the idea that female oppression, regardless of cultural or socio-economic circumstance, shall never be tolerated by atheists or freethinkers, nor should it be tolerated in general. It is a plague, and right alongside religious oppression of lifestyle, sexuality, and thought, has prevented the natural progression of society. It has been a detriment to mankind, and remains so. Therefore, it is only right to acknowledge the sexual abuse that has continually persisted within the culture of Islam. It is vital to understand that although every religious system has its documented benefits to the psychological and physiological well-being of human life, the adverse effects it has created out of its personal chaos supersedes them. The ongoing persecution of the freedom of women is only analogous to all else that is wrong with every religion, rather than Islam exclusively. It goes beyond the boundaries of what is acceptably *cultural*, and bleeds its atrocities into what is unacceptably *fundamentalist*.

In this world, rape remains a tool to not only subjugate women's identities and livelihoods, but also promote an utter contempt for their species. In the past, these things were minor social infractions based upon the severity of their implications. But in the modern age, especially in developed societies, this oppression has become a point of contention for most of the Western world. The main reasons for this are rooted in the fact that we have seen these atrocious acts played out in multiple other cultures to the same extent with identical results. Psychologists have acknowledged this form of abuse as a method of control, throwing to the side the typical "spoils of war" treatment given to the subject.

To be fair, it was not directly Muhammad that commended rape as a proper treatment for women captured in wartime. Technically, he was just the messenger; as we all know, "Thou shalt not shoot the messenger." Allah himself, or as we must refer to him for legal and safety purposes, "Allah the Exalted," essentially instituted this policy:

> Some of the Companions of the Apostle of Allah (may peace be upon him) were reluctant to have intercourse with the female captives in the presence of their husbands who were unbelievers. So Allah, the Exalted, sent down the Qur'anic verse: (Sura 4:24) "And all married women [are forbidden] unto you save those [captives] whom your right hands possess." (Abu Dawud 2150, also Muslim 3433)

So in essence there were, at first, inhibitions about whether they should go about raping the wives of the soldiers in front of them; this would be the humane thing to contemplate, as it would go against better judgment to do so. That internal "on-off" switch telling you the difference between right and wrong is disabled when you throw God into the mix. We are not to pretend that this is surprising; this is the same God, of course, that allowed the rape of women in Sodom and Gomorrah, so why should this instance be separate? It is also important to know that Allah only believed in the rape of "unbelievers," meaning those who were not Muslim.

This is only true historically, however. In the time in which these events occurred in the Qur'an, the Muslim community was in the deep minority. Therefore, rape was very abundant. In the modern age, rape occurs on an infrequent basis, but it is in the seedy underground of the Muslim world; that underground is approximately the same size as twelve New York sewer systems, but that is only a technicality. Commonly, women are raped for failing to adhere to directions given by certain over-excited males, and therefore, are prosecuted by the "legal system" of Islamic communities. Only in a place such as this would being raped actually get you persecuted over your offender.

The implications of these sexually abusive situations are grave. In a culture obsessed with virginity and pureness, being "unclean" can turn a woman into a social pariah. In many instances, it can lead to her death. The Muslim community is not very subtle about the way they execute women. The communal stoning technique, whereby they bury a woman up to the neck and have the public stone her slowly to death, is commonplace in strict Muslim societies. Women must acknowledge that they should be treated as livestock, dress the way a man has said they have to dress, and marry the person a man says they have to marry, and if they do not, then are pushed into "honor killings," which are believed to clear the family of any poor record it may have attained by one of its members sliding against their directives. Why did you think Muslim women should conveniently be covered from head to foot at all times? Muslims believe that if women didn't flaunt their "goods,", then they wouldn't get what was already coming to them.

Virginity in Islamic cultures is something that, even for a religion, remains a strangely disproportionate preoccupation. This is, naturally, only linked to the virginity of women; as in American cultures, a woman who spreads herself thinly is a "whore," but a man who does the same is "impressive." In Islam, as with the Mormons, a man can have many wives, but a wife just one man. Although this is banned by law in most civilized countries and goes against the majority of social practice, it remains the same. This fixation on virginity is enormously prevalent in the Qur'an itself. When Muslim men die and pass to Islamic Paradise (Heaven), they expect to enter a utopian dimension where wine, milk, and honey flow in excess. They will be greeted with 72 young virgin women of "perpetual freshness" (whatever that means). For eternity, they will be given an IV drip of Viagra: "a man in paradise shall be given virility equal to that of a hundred men."

Yet there is so much more with the infatuation with sex in heaven:

"They will recline (with ease) on thrones arranged in ranks. And We shall marry them to Huris (fair females) with wide lovely eyes" (Quran-52:17-20).

"...they will sit with bashful, dark-eyed virgins, as chaste as the sheltered eggs of ostriches" (Quran 37:40-48).

"Yes and we shall wed them to dark-eyed houris (beautiful virgins)" (Quran 44:51-55).

"In them will be bashful virgins neither man nor Jinn will have touched before. Then which of the favours of your Lord will you deny?" (Quran 55:56-57).

"As for the righteous, they surely triumph. Their gardens and vineyards and high-bosomed (pointed breast) virgins for companions, truly overflowing cup" (Quran 78:31-32).

"And young full-breasted (mature) maidens of equal age, and a full cup of wine" (Quran 78: 33-34).

"...we created the houris and made them virgins, loving companions for those on the right hand..." (Quran 56:34-37).

Doesn't this sound like paradise? Wouldn't you perform drastic measures, as a teenage male, or a twenty-something year old, to ensure this fate? Any man reading this knows that in his late teens and early twenties, the age of an average warrior in the 6th century, he may have thought that if he was going to die anyway, then he might as well move onto the afterlife and get this. If you as a teenage male had to decide between a Christian heaven of singing praise to god all day long and this, I think the choice would be pretty simple.

As a thought experiment, let's go through what Muhammad had to do in order to assure that his vision was clearly desired, and furthermore, fully adhered to in the manner he wanted. As a lover of suspense and action films, I have been toying around with a film plot. Humor me:

*It is 1955 in Russia. There is a masterful General named Vladomid. His strategy: create an army of sex-starved, imagination-ridden soldiers. His promise: a paradise where sex occurs on par like all are descended from rabbits. These ultimate soldiers are called Russlims, and there goal is to spread like wildfire and dominate the Euro-Asiatic continents. From birth they are told the story of paradise. Vladomid, however, covers up his females in an attempt to allow the Russlim imagination to run wild. With expectations high, the army is poised to do what it takes to achieve paradise. Alcohol, like women, is forbidden; in Paradise, however, it flows freely. He explains to them the glories of women, their shape and form, and the taste of the finest alcohols in the land. He explains the "purity," the virginity, of the women in Paradise; no man before has touched them, and they will be the first person that they have revealed themselves to. In order to do this, they must fight as hard as they can to eradicate not only Vladomid's arch nemesis, Christo, but also to propagate their agenda.*

It almost sounds like a James Bond film in reverse. Unfortunately, it represents a reality. Women do not get a paradise. They are given the option of following their husband (of choice!) to the after-life, only to be thrown aside for the 72 virginal women. However, they do have the opportunity to be renewed as virgins, so as to be acceptable by heavenly standards.

The covering up of women came from Muhammad's utter contempt for men gazing at his "possessions." His envious nature led him to promoting what he referred to as "hijab," roughly translated to "veiling," stemming from the Arabic "hijaba," meaning "hidden from view." It originated when Muhammad stumbled upon his many wives flirting with other men. At that instance, he ordered them to speak from behind a curtain, so as no man could lay eyes upon them. This also led to women not being allowed in the presence of men during prayer, and they must be secluded in a smaller room; some are relegated to the basement. It is believed that Muhammad found the sitting, bending, and prostrating to be distracting for men during prayer.

Rape is also a tool by which the Islamic nation keeps its congregation exclusively Middle-Eastern. Of course this is not an agenda that many will admit openly, and some honestly reject it, but it still occurs. As women are impregnated by members of their own communities, as well as survive the outcome, they give birth to pure-bred Muslims. We can refer to this as a method of "ethnic cleansing," which is reinforced by the obvious hatred Muslim absolutists have with the spread of Western culture. Since women are the exclusive method of long-term social reproduction, they are used as vehicles for this agenda. It is a method of destroying other communities and spreading the religion of Islam. Once again, this is one of the only mainstream religions that still do this in such a direct and abusive manner.

What is more horrific about the events beyond the events themselves is that these situations are arising in Western cultures. Religion tends to be migratory, and as Muslims migrate, so do their more extremist tendencies. Of course, just like any religion, there are some members who do not adhere to such beliefs. In fact, they represent the majority, and that is a good sign. However, until these events subside permanently, we must still discuss and bring them to the forefront. What must be gleaned from the progression of the oppressive forces in the Islamic movement is that once an individual obtains power (through religious authority or otherwise), they will oftentimes abuse this power. It is in this path that Muhammad chose to follow, and in this way, no different than the oppressive figures of our history.

I was a soldier in the Canadian army who was sent around the world for five years between 1988 until the end of 1992. I served in Germany when there was still a wall, served during the first Iraq war, during the Yugoslavian ethnic religious cleansing, Rwanda, Cyprus, and the Golan Heights. I know what it is like to be a soldier and so do many of my friends. You need something to look forward to; you need a justification as to why you are going to war, why you might have to kill people and why you may have to die. Fortunately I was, I hope, on the right side of the argument: to stop tyranny, stop ethnic cleansing, and prevent genocide. But the soldiers on the other side had their justifications for their actions, and still do today, and as every general and commander knows, leadership is the art of influencing human behavior.

Apart from the fact that a member of Islam's entire purpose, much as any religious entity, is to convert new members, there are consequences when those who were converted previously reject the religion openly. In Islamic culture, this is known as "apostasy," which is literally defined as to "relapse" or "regress." Naturally, this is related to the more orthodox religious practices of the Islamic world;

its graveness is noted in the consequences surrounding apostasy: death. I will be the first to describe the problems with extremist policies of this nature, as I live in a European country that is currently undergoing a tremendous socio-religious shift. The fear of Islamic control is palpable in my region, as it is in the rest of the Western world. The reason for this is that Islam has a set of cultural laws called "sharia." The controversy surrounding "sharia law" has been set in place by political, conservative bloggers and commentators, but as with every sensationalized bit of information, there is always something of real substance underneath it.

One instance of this occurring is in the city of Brussels, in Belgium, which is an absolutely amazing city and country with a rich cultural history. This includes being just a few kilometers from where Napoleon took his last stand, where the poem Flanders Fields comes from, and where the French fry was actually invented. Today, the largest religious group is Islam, which represents over 25% of the population and 40% of all school children. As other religions Europe-wide lose their flocks, the faith of Islam is growing and replacing them; today some actually refer to Brussels as "Belgistan" and the political landscape reflects it. There are places in Brussels where you will not see women without a head scarf and where Sharia Law is practiced indiscriminately. This is where the political movement is not about education, or the betterment of public infrastructure, but instead focuses on women not wearing certain articles of clothing, or that theft should be punished by the cutting off of hands, that stoning should be the law for adultery and that homosexuals should be put to death. By 2030, Muslims with their birth rate will have an absolute majority in Brussels, the European capital. Although they may believe that democracy is in direct opposition to the agenda of their culture, they certainly know how to use democracy to achieve their goals. Once again, the non-believer is forced to tolerate religious extremism.

At the end of the day, the thoughts of every Brussels citizen must be related to what happens when these radical, extremist Islamic ideologies begin to bleed into their political infrastructure. If you rationalize this, you can easily see that the voting population will inevitably become heavily Muslim by nature. The possibility for the more extremist, orthodox policymaking in the future becomes prevalent. These are not simply assumptions; this is something that is occurring as I type these very words. What will happen to the culture of Belgium when ordinances are passed allowing leniency for the persecution of homosexuals, women, and minorities? The answer: a religiously tolerant society will become exactly the opposite.

After World War II, Europe was in shambles because of an ideology that one type of people were superior to all the others, and rebuilding Europe, the countries, and the cities was going to be no simplistic feat. There are literally hundreds of books on the subject, so I ask that you please excuse me for belittling the work of so many others in this paragraph, but essentially every country needed the few workers they had to make bread, deliver milk, run factories, and make clothes and every single person who could work was employed to capacity. The problem is that there were not enough *native* workers to work the factories or rebuild the nations; so many countries offered people of *other* countries a chance to be a guest worker. Since the Martial Plan ensured that there was a free and secured flow of money pegged against the US dollar, guest workers realized that they could make a lot of money in another country and send that money home to take care of their own families. For example, the Germans offered the Italians and Turkish people guest work, and the Belgians offered the Moroccans the same, and each country profited from cheap labor. For the governments at the time, religion from each corresponding nation never played a role. Today, however, the decisions of sixty years ago have never been more important.

The final culmination of events was that Muslim immigrants migrated from their respective countries into the European continent. It is only natural that, after years of doing so, their culture would diffuse into Europe's. As we have seen with the United States, this is never *exclusively* a negative occurrence. However, as with illegal immigration coming from Mexico, things have been infinitely complicated, and furthermore, cultures may potentially become compromised in their wake.

What is important to remember about Islam is that it is a fascist ideology with a side of religious zealotry. Islam is not a tolerant religion by any means in the same sense as a Catholic is "tolerant" toward a Protestant. At its core, it is in direct conflict with democracy. To make one thing very clear there is no distinct difference between Islam, being a Muslim, and Sharia Law in the orthodoxy of the Islamic people; they are one and the same. Muslims believe that Allah makes the laws, not the people, and Allah tells the people what is right and what is wrong; what is allowed and what is forbidden. If a true Muslim follows the Qur'an, they will have no choice but to choose Islam and Sharia over democracy. To have truly democratic Sharia Law-based Muslims is an oxymoron. A Muslim must do what *Allah* says, rather than what the *people* say is respectful, moral, or right, and any Muslim who is against Sharia law cannot be a true follower of Islam.

In order to combat the spread of religious fanaticism without sounding trite but whilst reiterating the purpose of this book, we must put an end to it. In order to maintain this, we must prevent even the smallest of advancements of religion bleeding into State. This could be any religious symbol sneaking into the cracks, be it a publically-funded cross or burqa, that could topple years of social progress. The respective governments of Brussels and those other capitols, regions, and countries that face religious fundamentalism on such an immense scale will be the individual entities responsible for such prevention. They must teach in the classrooms the potential and actual devastation caused by religious fundamentalism; politicians must put away their apologist nature in order to deal with the issues at hand. Without this, there is potential for an all-out "Holy War" between the Western world and the oppressive factions of Islam.

# CHAPTER 14
## Other Religions

*When I told the people of Northern Ireland that I was an atheist, a woman in the audience stood up and said, "Yes, but is it the God of the Catholics or the God of the Protestants in whom you don't believe?"*

*Quentin Crisp*

Since I consider myself a fair debater, and to further the interest of our objective nature, I will spend some time talking about other religions alongside the traditional Abrahamic fixtures. This is more for the interest of other religions than for the atheist themselves, as fundamentalism runs strong in many religious facets. I personally do not believe that there is much debate to be had in the academic circles about the following religions, but regardless, it seems unethical not to bring up their seedier aspects. To note something very important: these religions generally pose a minimal threat to the freethinking humanist, but still retain older traditions that prove to be detrimental to the relevant people involved. Therefore, I will not waste too much time on either, but rather as done before, provide a case study from each religion as an example of how relatively motivational, peaceful religions can prove to hold darker elements within their borders; this is mainly for all of the apologist-humanist individuals who feel that religion has only *specific* varietals which remain dangerous or volatile. I can assure you, mysticism in almost every form doesn't maintain its floodwaters within a delicately maintained levy.

As I have mentioned previously, or at least can be inferred by now, I am natively a Canadian citizen but live in Germany with my family. Even though I am not an official citizen of Germany, I am still held under its legal system's rules. Due to Germany's history, any time people express an opinion of the Jewish culture or religion, eggshells can't even be *tiptoed* on or around. These opinions are encountered by a very large, pro-Jewish community (possibly out of guilt) and also by the unfortunate antithetical neo-Nazi movement, which also has a strong but small community. For the purpose of this book, I would like to note that overall, I do not have any real contention with the Jewish religion. I want to acknowledge that this is not out of fear of government reprimand, but rather personal experience and understanding of where their religion is *today*.

There is almost no need for me to argue against the Jewish religion as I have already done it debating the Old Testament and its wrongs, but I will be the first at the front of any march which promotes the diversity of culture and traditions which should not be lost. In the media, you rarely hear of the Jewish suicide bomber[35]. In Israel there is freedom of religion: you can be a Jew or as the old slogan promotes, Jew*ish*; it is even possible to live in Israel, be Jewish, and not believe in God, with no threat of death or disenfranchisement. I have a friend who is moderately Jewish. One of his kids wears a hat and doesn't shave his temples, and his other kid is an atheist. However, the atheist still plays the part when he goes home for holidays, not out of belief, but out of tradition. Christians may argue that their belief system *is* their tradition, but this is nonsense. In the Jewish faith there is no immediate threat to my family, and although there are many Jews all over the world, you do not see them fighting for the right to have the entire country celebrate or recognize their holidays, nor a mass-market week long shopping spree in promotion of it; you never see (serious) Jewish bumper stickers saying "let's keep the "Han" in Hanukkah.

I have a problem with fanatics within *any* religion, but out of the great majority of religious people, I have yet to see a surplus of Jewish extremists outside Israel. It is very rare, for instance, to see a gaggle of Jewish men come knocking on my door trying to convince me that they have the answers to mankind's infinite problems; nor do I ever see a Jewish male (barring the conflict in Israel, which I refuse

---

[35] Before my critics say it, yes I know: On October 18, 1983, a suicide bomber strapped with explosives was caught in the spectators' gallery of the US House of Representatives, attempting to blow up the US Capitol. The terrorist was a Jewish Israeli named 'Israel Rabinowits'.

to bring into this book's parameters) commit acts of terrorism, particularly in the Western world. For all intents and purposes, talking about the Jewish faith in this book is both to reinforce their (unfortunate) influence on the Christian religions that came from its initial teachings, as well as a "Thank You" for never using my tax dollars to attempt to convert me to Judaism. If most religions operated as the Jewish communities do, at least from my vantage point, we would have far less conflict with issues like separating Church and State, ritualistic praying before events, or intense door-to-door proselytizing. These are generally irrelevant to the Jewish populace.

And of course, we could talk about all their strange quirks, but that is not the point of this book. Atheists don't have a problem with Jews simply because they leave us alone, and that is what we want. If you want to believe in an all-powerful deity, you should have the freedom to do it, but keep it out of my space, as we don't need to see it, and we certainly don't need to hear about it. So to that, I would like to ask all other religions—the extremist Muslim who will threaten those who don't acknowledge the prophet Mohammed, the Christians who want me to believe that Jesus is my savior, and the Jehovah's Witnesses and Mormons who come knocking on my door—to take a lesson from the Jewish faith. They are a religion of tradition, rather than radical fundamentalist belief.

In a relevant parallel, no one would *ever* think (excluding a few Christian radicals) that the Cheyenne Native Americans, for instance, should not practice their language or traditions and dances; or that the Sechelt Indians from my hometown should not practice their own version of law and self-government; or that the aborigines of Australia shouldn't be allowed to teach their children about their ancestry and tradition. To do so, as a member of the human species, would be to lose that most important part of our being called history, and (most of us) would even opt to paying for it with tax dollars because it represents our diverse cultural dynamics. But there has never been a Cheyenne or Sechelt Native American tribe, or an aborigine from Australia, preaching that if I don't follow him and my family doesn't follow them, then I will consequently burn in Hell (or Mordor) as punishment forever. So to solidify my point, we will shift our focus away from these infinitely peaceful, isolated populations and move on to potentially dangerous elements of passive religions.

## The Dali Lama and the Buddhists

I have been to China over twenty-five times, and have worked with companies in the north in Shenyang as well as to the south in Guangzhou. In between, I have actually been a consultant to the Chinese government delegation from Taiyuan, and even had the daughters of a Chinese mayor of Chángzhì at my house for Christmas. Other than actually holding a Communist Party Pass in my wallet, I understand China deeply, and potentially much better than most people. Yet when you go to China as a Westerner, processing only one side of the story, you tend to believe it. I have stayed with business owners at their homes and, over my lifetime, have done millions of dollars' worth of work together with my Chinese partners and continue to do so today.

I have a friend in China from Tibet, and in the beginning, I never wanted to bring up the long Tibetan history of Chinese invasion. However, after a long night and a few beers, I presented my questions; unfortunately, it was in the presence of his natively Chinese acquaintance. Would you have thought the two of them would have begun fighting, like a Palestinian and a Jew? Like a Native American and a soldier from Custard's army? Like a Catholic and a Protestant in Northern Ireland? Before I give you a complete history of the conflict, I want to foreword it by explaining that very few Tibetans, outside of the monks, ever *yearn* for the days gone by, and most of the Tibetans actually *thank* the Chinese for doing what they did. So the next time you hear a story about the Dali Lama, Tibet, and Buddhism I want you remember this:

In 1950, China's "People's Liberation Army" entered Tibet, destroying the measly, sporadic resistance on behalf of Tibet. By 1951, Tibet had already begun deliberations with China on China's sovereignty over Tibet. The end result was the "Seventeen Points" agreement, an abridged title of a relatively unnecessary mouthful. In the "treaty," for lack of a better term, China preserved Tibetan ways of life in exchange for its cooperation in the Chinese occupation of Tibet, as well as the allowance of eventually altering certain aspects of the Tibetan town for use of military forces. Naturally, there was some general opposition from the primary authorities in Tibet: the Dali Lama and his monastery-based flock. By 1959, in fact, he had gone as far as repudiating the agreement, arguing that those involved were under "duress" by the Chinese government to make a decision. Although many people involved explained things under a different light, monk opposition still persisted.

As a frame of reference to what Tibetan life was before the Chinese government invaded its walls, or before Hollywood and some of its actors took up the cause in helping Tibet, we will discuss some of the societal structures practiced by Tibetan religious authority. First and foremost, Tibet and China have an incredibly long history of conflict, so we will spare the majority of these circumstantial details as they could fill the pages of a book on their own accord. Buddhism in Tibet, which is the true cultural sculptor at hand, is a fairly new religion compared to its older Abrahamic counterparts. Its first recorded appearance was approximately the 5th century CE. Since it was written in Sanskrit, the first translation happened to be in Tibetan, which explains its regional origins. The foundation of what is now modern day Buddhism, and the concern of this segment, came from the practice of "monasticism," which is simply the use of monasteries as place of worship and central cultural-religious forums.

There were many "Lamas" in Tibet, but there is only one "Dalai Lama"; you can imagine the Dalai Lama and his Lamas similarly to the Pope and the Bishops. It was set up just like the Catholic Church. The first Dalai Lama was put into power by the Chinese army in 1391 and he lived until 1474. The concept of "reincarnation" evolved from the need to keep power in the family with the strongest leader, in the same way that kings and queens pass on their power to their children, and as much as the parents of successful companies put their children in charge; for a more metaphysical example, in the same way as saying my son is a reincarnation of me. Reincarnation is a motivational tool for the members of Buddhism, and a way of justifying power; for instance, in his struggle for power, the first Dalai Lama destroyed Monasteries and destroyed texts, which was contrary to his claim that he was the reincarnation of Buddha.

It wasn't really until the fifth generational Dalai Lama in 1617 that things really started to become interesting for the Tibetan people and their new (forced) belief system. I will not spend a great deal of time on Buddhism itself, but rather the circumstances surrounding its use and influence; if you want to read more about the facts, there are many well-researched books out there which the Dalai Lama isn't so proud of, such as books on reincarnation, which was inevitably used to further the gap between social classes. The fifth Dalai Lama unified the country and all the monasteries under his personal political and social philosophies, and started what Richard Gere might claim to be "Heaven on Earth," but what the Tibetan people, up until 1959, a lesser replication of modern day North Korea. The land did not belong to the people, the people had no say in the happenings of Tibet, and the land belonged to the monasteries and the Tibetan militia.

Most of the people who worked the land, even up to 1959 were slaves (serfs). Pradyumna Karan even admitted that "a great deal of real estate belonged to the monasteries, and most of them amassed great riches.[36]" This was not the Tibet of Hollywood; this was a virtual nightmare for its people. Since the majority of the land was owned by monasteries, they were really just land barons. Calling them monasteries, however, gives them some kind of godly blessing, as opposed to calling them castles with princes, doesn't it? Call them monasteries with monks and they have godly authority to do what they want. The serfs could not vote, and they could not run away, for if they did, the monks would chop off limbs, cut out tongues if someone spoke against them, poke out eyes, even slash hamstrings. The serfs were also kept subdued by their own religious beliefs, as violence was out of the question for lesser beings.

How could the Buddhist monks justify these actions, and subsequently, condone slavery? Reincarnation. The serfs must have done something really atrocious in another life, and for that, they are being punished in this one, and it is the *perfect* scheme isn't it? But the monks and the ever-loving Dalai Lama promised that if the serfs did what the monks said and worked for them until their eventual demise, in exchange, the serf's next life would be unimaginably better; isn't reincarnation great? As I always say, religious leaders, *including* the Dalai Lama, get everything they want in this life by promising everything you could possibly want in the next one. The history of Tibet proves to be no exception to this timeless rule.

As an example of the religious authority's demands from the Tibetan people, I have provided a concise list of just some of the taxes placed on the already downtrodden populace as provided to me

[36] The changing face of Tibet: the impact of Chinese Communist ideology on the landscape University Press of Kentucky, 1976

by my Tibetan friend which was told to him from his very own grandfather:

- Begging tax.
- Tax for marriage.
- Tax for each child birth.
- Tax for planting a new tree.
- Dancing tax.
- Celebration tax.
- Bell-ringing tax.
- Tax for going to jail.
- Tax for getting out of jail.
- Tax for unemployment.

Now if the average serf who worked for nothing to begin with, as over 80% of the population did, could not afford the tax the Dalai Lama and his monasteries enforced, they would lend the serf the money. This seems rather generous until the serfs would look at the fine print. Like any enterprise, there were some "hidden fees," to put things lightly. The loans came with interest rates of up to 50%, and if that could not be paid back in the designated time frame, then the tax would be passed onto that person's family forever, keeping them in debt to the monastery. Naturally, this debt would amount to more serfdom from the remaining family and the generations to come. Certainly the old aristocracy wants China out of Tibet, as they want to go back to the old system, where the monks could do as they pleased and had the power to go about their business of slavery, corruption, and greed.

Today, Tibet enjoys many more benefits than are publicised; it is not a black-and -white case of "China Bad," "Dalai Lama Good." China installed not only physical alterations to the landscape and town, such as running water and irrigation systems, but also new secular, moral infrastructure while maintaining the aspect of life Tibetans were used to. For a look at new moral codes, simply ask the Tibetan or his grandson who no longer belongs to the cyclical slave-trade anymore.

It is an important lesson to understand that one should never take "one side" of the coin for granted; often times, "tails" is just as

166 of 212 "Born Again Atheist"

important to hedge your bets against as the more favourable "heads."
As Westerners, we tend to accept our typical ways of living whilst
rejecting, wholly, other potential aspects of the economy, for
instance, simply because we are *used* to the ways in which things
operate. As an example, look at how we view communism even
today. I find it "funny" that we can view what the Western world has
done in the Middle-East in the last decade, invading a culture and
attempting to change it from the inside out, and then immediately
view what China did in Tibet as tyrannous and horrific. It goes to
explain a mind-set by which a culture can be *brainwashed* in believing
certain authority is more just, or validated, at reigning than another of
equal but different proportions; sort of like the difference between
Christianity and non-belief.

## Those Calm Like Hindu Cows

Following the Buddhist comes their (somewhat) cousin, Hindu.
It is hard pressing to find a particular instance in which we can relate
them to the Buddhists in such a negative light as the Buddhists have
presented themselves. However, there *is* one thing that I can discuss:
Hindus use the caste system. If you are unfamiliar with this form of
social order, I will describe it in the most *lay* terms imaginable: some
individuals are born into wealth, and others are born into filth. This
sounds similar to Western culture, whereby a family of generational
wealth births others into their wealth, with the same being true for
poverty. However, in Hindu culture, this is an *institutional* practice,
which means that there is a certain amount of *control* over who is
wealthy and who is not.

It is important to note that although the caste system is not
indigenous to the Hindu religion, it remains embraced by the religion.
The caste system actually has its roots in British colonial culture,
whereby its Indian acquirement was due to the British rule in India at
the time. Many scholars argue that the system must be looked at from
two different perspectives: the ideological and the implemented. To
begin with the ideological is to look at a highly complex organism.
Ideologically the caste system introduces five main castes, which
continuously branch off into hundreds of sub-groups that further
themselves into more *localized* sub-groups. The more specific groups

are the boundaries people base their marriage, work, and economic status around.

A man named Ambedkar, who was an Indian native, wrote extensively on the subject of the social and emotional constraints placed upon him by the caste system. According to Ambedkar, castes apportioned the population, only to disintegrate and cause myriad divisions, further isolating people and causing confusion. Even the upper caste, the Brahmin, segmented itself and crumbled. The curse of caste, according to Ambedkar, split the Brahmin priest class into well over 1400 sub-castes. Furthermore, many view the caste system as a mass-economic sanction on the Indian population. It provided a structure and validation by which the upper level castes could exploit the lower level castes for whatever they saw fit; typically, it would be a form of serfdom similar to how the Buddhists implemented their variations of slavery. However, the Hindus were paid, although relatively little in comparison.

## Karma as a Redemptive Property

I know this might be hard for anyone to believe, but I do think there is a form of karma, and as an atheist, we must almost wish that these religious ideologies of yin and yang and karma were true; wouldn't you just love to see the religious authority getting a taste of their own medicine? Naturally, this karma would have nothing to do with a supreme being, but with nature itself: pure Darwinian karma. A scientist, a skeptic, and an atheist must believe that every action gets a reaction; where there is matter, there is anti-matter. We know this to be true, and where there is an action there is a reaction. But do not misunderstand me; this is not metaphysical, but scientific. I am not speaking of some hocus-pocus. I do believe that there will be a time in our future where the religions of today will be looked upon like those of the great god Horus, Zeus, and Jupiter, and I know that day will come. Oh yes I believe in karma, but in a Darwinian sense. Atheism will always survive because it is the fittest. There is no reason to believe anyone is pulling the strings. You are in full control of your own destiny, and if you murder someone, you should and most likely will be punished, and not by some god, but by society. If someone rapes someone else, it is wrong, and society knows it, and the police and the justice system will inevitably prevail. DNA testing has done more for our Darwinian karma than any god in the sky. Today, as opposed to when religion ruled in Europe, there are now fewer than 2 murders per 100,000 people according to the UNODC[37].

That is yin and yang, that is Karma, but it is thanks to science, not god or a strange energy. People who do wrong will be caught (of course, some will not), but the belief in Darwinian karma is the belief that you will get what you deserve. For the fanatic Christian, their karma will be that there is no god; for the Muslim, that there is no paradise filled with virgins; for the Mormon, no planet to dominate; for the Jehovah's Witness, they will not wake up in Paradise. As for me, nothing will happen to me, as I am a good father, and a faithful husband. I donate to charities that actually help people without a religious agenda, without disclosing my name. Do you know what I will get in return? I already have it: a great wife, superb children, a wonderful career, and the occasional hate mail threatening my family while wishing us eternal hellfire. This is not because I did anything to them personally, nor their families, but because I refused to accept their god. There is no magical energy in this world other than the one you create. And if enough of us atheists stop tolerating their secular intolerance (not just for *some*), that is energy; that is real, and this is the true essence of Darwin: survival of the fittest was never "survival of those who kept their mouth clamped down and did what the strongest, the richest, loudest or fastest or the ones with the tallest hats wanted us to do." Survival of the fittest is about change, sometimes due to chance, but mostly due to adaptation. You can help people change when we get the chance by not making you adapt to what they want. I call that Darwinian karma.

## Newer Religions

Religions have come and they have gone. That is without question. At one point in time, a religious concept was that the Sun was actually a god. I am sure many people have heard of Ra, the Egyptian god. We now laugh at the Egyptian theory of Ra, but it is no different than many of the mythologies we hold true today. When considering other religions, it is most important to acknowledge not

---

[37] United Nations Office on Drugs and Crime

what is *already* established, but what will inevitably pose as a dangerous religious authority in the future. As with all previously established religions, there needs to be a starting-off point. It is not like Jesus Christ never had to preach the word of God for Christianity to spread as widely and rapidly as it did. There was a concerted effort and a strategy behind it all. Scientology is a great example of a religion that spread through influence, coming from the already popular science fiction author, L. Ron Hubbard, and spreading over the last forty years. Now that Hollywood has picked it up as its unofficial *in vogue* religion, it has spread into quite a large spotlight in the religious arena.

Of course, many people dismiss scientology as a cult. Many of these individuals are also involved in a cult themselves; today, the cult is now acceptably mainstream. Christianity, the world's largest religion, had its roots in a similar cultural landscape. It was not easy for Christ and his followers to start the religion (he was crucified for it, if you do not remember). So when it comes to the hypocrisy of saying such a thing, we can only provide the latter testimonial. In order to predict further religious invasions from whatever particular local society tomorrow, we must see how the leaders of these groups have developed their philosophies, as well as enacted them with some finesse. They were, of course, naturally able to convince the world that Christianity is the light, Islam is by nature peaceful, and furthermore, convince Richard Gere that Buddhism is the way out; the last example is infinitely more *dastardly*, if you could not catch my drift.

The fact that individuals are infinitely malleable means that there will always be people of charisma to sculpt them. As an example, it took only seconds for Charles Manson to convince each of his young "disciples" to join his desert commune. After he was in, the rest of the horrid events followed suit. The situations invented by Hubbard and Christ are no different. As any psychologist will tell you, there is a basic structure to religious authority (which is synonymous to their theories on cult behavior) that is consistently in the picture. In order to give some structure to this subchapter, I will go through the mode of describing this structure:

1) The cult must express interest in providing its followers with the "ultimate" answer to existence. This could be

like the Heaven's Gate cult, who believed that the Earth was going to be recycled (presumably by God, as he is a master recycler), and they were to leave the Earth before that. Since they had this knowledge, then they had "divine" insight into the end of the world. They intended to leave the Earth (by suicide, as their bodies were only a "vessel") beforehand, and come back to it as a hugely specialized, intelligent population.

2)    The cult must have an incredibly charismatic leader. I am not talking about "Billy Mays" charismatic; we are not concerned with excitability, although it helps. We are talking about "Adolf Hitler" charismatic. This requires conviction, whether it be shouting your beliefs from a mountain or pounding your fists in the audience's general direction. In order to truly manipulate, the leader has to believe that *he* and he alone holds the truth.

3)    The cult must, as an extension of "2," abuse the knowledge that the leader has the truth. At the end of the day, the cult will yearn to know it, and they will be under absolute control. Although Manson never truly had a purpose, as his massacre was based on juvenile revenge, his believers felt purposeful in taking the lives of others.

4)    After the control is established, the leader will then be infallible. From Christ came God, and not the other way around. As soon as Christ established himself as a leader and his followers saw him as infallible, he was able to manipulate them; now that Christ is gone, his counterpart "God" has taken over the status of infallible. If you cannot achieve all of the subsequent elements of a cult, then you will be without the fourth element. If you do not have the fourth element, all else crumbles in its wake. Criticism must not be tolerated in the cult; as soon as authority is questioned, the dominoes begin to fall.

Now that we understand these elements, we can easily apply them to an upcoming cult that has just recently (in the last thirty years) begun to take shape. The leader of this cult is named Theodor Geisel. His followers have come to know him by his pseudonyms, "The Rosetta Stone" and "Theo LeSieg." Some of them translate the latter literally into "The Theology That Wins." Hundreds of thousands of copies of his scriptures have been transcribed, mailed, gifted, and widely read by millions of people across the world. He has entered the lives of many, but most importantly, that of children.

This is my largest concern about The Theologian Geisel. In his lifetime, he had painstakingly and meticulously painted steps to indoctrinate unknowing children to his cause. When you begin to think about his philosophy from a marketing point of view, it is *perfect*. Do not use the parents; rather, go directly for the children. He has developed an idea for programming children before their parent's own eyes, actually skipping the middle man. It is genius and madness at the same time, and it is surprising that I am probably the first person ever to write about it. Of the hundreds of thousands of people and children worldwide who have heard his message in some way or another, it amazes me that there has been no news coverage, no backlash, and no discrediting.

His method is synonymous to all other religious authoritarian figures. He found a market by which he could proliferate his words and philosophies, and gave hope to those that needed it in particular points in history. By doing so, he created a name for himself, accrediting not only his talents as a storyteller but as an influence on children. He took what St. Francis Xavier, the Jesuit Missionary, said to heart: "[g]ive me the child until he is seven and I'll give you the man." By grabbing his audience early, he could instill all of his philosophy into them by the time they were older, and if he were lucky, could inevitably be able to control some of their very thoughts.

He wrote many political musings as well as religious. Some people may come to know his work in the future as spawning much debate between conservative and liberal groups; he *has* been known to shake even the thickest trees, after all. His theory he labelled "The Lorax" spurred vehement reactions from conservatives on the theories of regulating environmentalism. What is mainly concerning, especially to me as a parent, is how *easy* it was for him to bypass my defenses, letting him into the lives of my children. Here are a few quotes to describe what I am referring to:

*"Today is your day! Your mountain is waiting."*
*"Adults are just obsolete children and the hell with them."*
*"Be yourself, because those who matter don't mind, and those who mind don't matter. To the world you may be one person; but to one person you may be the world."*

So not only do we have to confront the notion that children should have their own *identities*, but that they should also question authoritarian figures. Since they are so young, the primary figures of authority in their lives are, unsurprisingly, mainly their parents; although there are teachers in their everyday lives, the parents still forced them into that position. If the children were to start not only feeling independent interpersonally, but also of their own parents, then it is possible that, as the last quote illuminates, they could become entirely *indifferent* to societal pressures and insecurities. Last but not least, this could cultivate roots for rebellious creativity, energy, and worst of all, give a purpose to their lives.

If you are not ignorant of the literary world, then you would have realized immediately that the person I am talking about goes by the pen name Dr. Suess. If you are ignorant of *sarcasm* as a literary mechanism, then I will tell you now that I don't believe anything I have said about the late, great Geisel. In fact, I am a personal fan of Dr. Suess, and my children have learned from him some very important issues pertaining to morality. However, I must explicitly note to those of faith: we can turn any written word into scripture, and if I was serious about Dr. Suess, I would be able to spin his words into much deeper things than originally intended, thereby spawning a potential "philosophy of Dr. Suess." If I took more time than I would ever choose to, we could easily convince people that Suess' words were the foundation of something infinitely, universally greater. At the end of the day, we have ourselves a religion.

If I were to actually go about the process of interchanging the fables in the Bible with the fables that Geisel created, could you imagine how well some of them would match up? The language, of course would need to be entirely rewritten in order to be understood in the archaic languages of the Bible itself, but the stories, morally, would match up almost perfectly. Perhaps today we would traditionally gorge on green eggs and ham come Thanksgiving; perhaps our Santa Clause would have the opposite job of actually *taking from* us, rather than giving. Certain aspects of our culture would completely vanish, which goes to show just how deep religious modes of thought have embedded themselves in our culture.

The tales from both the Bible and Suess hold relevant tales of morality, as well; Suess, however, is entirely more applicable today than the Bible is. How could we *possibly* find controversy in something like "The Butter Battle Book," whose whole purpose was to explain how silly it was to argue over on which side of the toast one puts butter? This is a reference to the Cold War, where our nuclear armament was a glorified pissing contest. This is a much better life lesson than, say, Sodom and Gomorrah. In the least, it is much less terrifying. "The Cat in the Hat" was almost the *opposite* of Sodom and Gomorrah in some ways. The cat was a complete nuisance to the two protagonists, and they still allowed him to roam about their house without a question. Interchange the cat with a homosexual, and there would be people who would shoot him on sight, simply for being the wrong type in the wrong location.

At the end of the day, we should be able to tell fairy tales. Children *should* listen to the musings of *Green Eggs and Ham*, Jonah and the Whale, *Ponocchio*, and even Jesus Christ, if we leave out the more gruesome details. It is when *adults*, not children, begin to take these stories as a literal truth that problems begin to arise. If people would have misconstrued Aesop's fables to the point where they were to literally move as slowly as a tortoise in hopes to beat the faster hare (although in some places this is relevant; take heed, United States), then I am sure he would have given up hope on writing them at all. If the story of Jack and the Beanstalk is told to a child, that child generally understands that there is no real beanstalk that leads to the skies. Told to an adult and said that, without a doubt, it was divine inspiration from God, the results would be dramatically different.

Not one single individual on this earth should have personal issues with teaching morality through fictional stories, and Aesop should *never* have had to fear that his stories would be taken for more than they were worth; as I know of now, none have, but who knows what's to come. This is applicable to being a member of *any* religious affiliation, or for some of us, non-religious. The stories are told as anecdotal morality tales, but furthermore, give historians and the public great insight into culturally rich times in our world. The point of accentuating this so particularly is because the stories in the Bible began as fables themselves. The writers of the Bible were nothing more than common plagiarists. Sumerian, Babylonian, and Egyptian cultures created the creative frameworks for the Bible's stories. It just took a handful of individuals to plug in catchy names that they created, and from there, began a game of fill-in-the-blank.

# CHAPTER 15
## *Conclusions*

*"The only people who have the right to claim any sort of born again status are Atheists"*

*Lance Gregorchuk*

In a strange, almost *omniscient* way, I feel that if I polled a considerable number of people on the street, most of them would agree on the more extremist views on religion—extremist in the ways people take some improbable nonsense as literal truth, such as the talking snake, Noah's Ark, or perhaps sinning by wanting their lawn to look like their neighbor's. Most individuals would not side with many of these stories and anecdotes today. Rather, they would take them with a grain of salt. They may even question their importance, maybe in context with history. In all likeliness, however, and what amazes me is that they will still retain the traditional Christian outlook of Heaven and Hell, Jesus Christ, and the man we know as God. For the most part, this book is intended for those people.

As you know, this book was not for the people who take the Bible as infallible—as a literal, binding truth. These are the individuals who hold grave consequence in their ideologies. They have controlled numerous sects of society through religious propagation, spreading their roots into our political, moral, social, and authoritarian societal fabrics. This form of fanaticism, as proven in the previous chapters, will lead and has led to numerous instances of violence, persecution, and worst of all, intellectual mutiny. It is to these people that will not read my book but will nevertheless judge it and wish me and my family, although we have done nothing to them except challenge their intellect, an eternity of pain and suffering, to whom I personally dedicate this final chapter.

To have a true *ideology*, one has to craft it. For those who subscribe to religious ideology, it has been crafted for them through hundreds of years and generations of people getting things wrong. As much as anything else, this remains true; for religion, however, infinitely more bloodshed and scientific regression can be found in its massive grave of worn policies and philosophies. It is not an *interpretation* of scripture that make people do whatever they do in the name of their god; it is exactly word for word what is written in scripture that makes religious people do crazy things, pass insane laws, hinder science, subjugate women, abuse children, commit genocide or honor killings, and be racists bigots, and intolerant at the end of the day. It has now become a war of being staunchly decisive about decisions past. Written word has now become increasingly strong, solidified by generations of people carrying on tradition without question. Unfortunately for the rest of us, this has led to terrible mistakes by understandably confused individuals.

As to not entirely beat the events of September 11th as one would a dead horse, the Islamic perpetrators, fell into the realm of confused individuals making terrible mistakes. Most religious scholars point to this flaw as a fundamental "misinterpretation" of the Qur'an. They argue that it is actually a relatively peaceful text. Yet you do not need to search very hard to find something much more sinister. If any layperson reads the Qur'an it is simple to illuminate the text as that which promotes ethnic purity (inevitably ethnic cleansing), misogyny, nationalism, and ideological fundamentalism. This ambiguity is what has faltered the Islamic culture in recent years from becoming more "mainstream," albeit its growing congregations. This ambiguity is what created atrocious acts that have devastated innumerable innocent lives and families.

We cannot use "interpretation" interchangeably with what is actually *written*, definitively and concisely, in the texts of the religious. Doing so would simply *forgive* the years of female oppression, homosexual persecution, and scientific intolerance, to highlight a few of the more severe issues plaguing our society today. It is what is *written* that provides both the thesis (and scientific antithesis) to stem cell research, for instance. This is a perfect example of an institutionally religious policy that has weeded itself indiscriminately into the public domain. It is known that stem cell research has extreme potential to either save or improve the lives of millions of individuals. Their arguments, although consisting of an array of possible points, lead to one outcome: doctors and scientists should not "play God," as they say. Well this argument would be valid if God actually "played God" as he should. It is not the free-will of individuals to lose a limb due to a flesh-eating bacteria; they cannot be held accountable. It is because of the medical community that these instances are not only treated and the life of that individual is improved, but they also help to prevent further occurrences.

Imagine if this same argument was posed for polio, cancer, Parkinson's, or the other hundreds of millions of diseases and mutations that God has so graciously blessed us with; it was by his poor design that these things (as a religious man views it) exist, after all. Where would we be? Well, first and foremost, there would be much fewer of us. Whether or not you find that a good thing is irrelevant. What is pertinent is the fact that what preceded death was human suffering. Could it be that God is that sadistic to create viruses whereby your entire internal system of organs hemorrhages? Furthermore, without the scientific advances in medicine so adamantly opposed by our imaginary situation, we would be living somewhere in the Middle Ages by now. That is hardly a place in which any modern citizen wishes to find themselves.

The reason that these thoughts have ever existed is because religious authorities thrived in times of desperation. So when individuals were sick with the Black Plague, they were infinitely more willing to succumb to their every will in order to be better. This is why they don't fret about disabling medical science with insane fervor. This current situation is synonymous to all of the cliché moments where parents describe to their children how society is much worse off than when they had been children themselves; more than likely, they would give anything to once again attend Woodstock, protest against "the man," and smoke and consume copious amounts of illicit narcotics. What parents and the religious authorities fail to truly understand, however, is that "progression" is not always *harmful*; just in as much as "different" is not always *bad*.

Even after faced with mountains of overwhelming evidence, however, flocks of people continue to maintain tradition, mainly because their parents instilled such values in them. As an adolescent, we rebel against our parents; as an adult, we find ourselves precisely trailing their life's trajectory. Therefore, institutions like marriage to be blessed before God, baptism to wash the child's sins away, confirmation or religious education are now done autonomously without question. Yet, maybe this is not done as thoughtlessly as one would assume. Could it be that those who do it are simply "hedging up their bet"? Perhaps they are not taking any chances in the gamble between eternal life and reason. It is, of course, much easier to donate to churches, baptize and confirm your child, mutilate his or her genitals at birth, and attempt to seek "forgiveness" for past indiscretions than risking all of the implications. As a man who values reason, this is pure insanity. It is certainly insanity if we consider our moral code validated by one man's book or another.

This atheism is not a system of "belief." I may be one of the few that out of sheer *probability* knows there is no God. I do not put blind input into this ideology, however. Nor will I go out of my way to compile farfetched notions of *why* there is no God. I have utilized decades of research, experience, and specialization in particular areas to come to this understanding. I for one do not own a fence to sit on, as these religious people do. It is this form of thinking that is, to say the least, despicable. These are the sort of individuals who remember not to use the Lord's name in vain (sometimes); who go out of their way to avoid pushing a button on an elevator Saturday or Sunday (every now and then); who pray before bed (about once a month). It is not only this intellectual laziness that poses a problem. If there is lenience in how far certain people take their religiosities, there is also certain boundaries (or lack thereof) as to the extremities by which they take form.

Certainly there are people who lean toward non-belief, such as agnostics, that may not partake in any form of religious ritual. Nor do they even ascribe their beliefs to religion in general. These people generally take the "May or May Not" approach to theistic possibility. Many great scientists throughout the generations, such as Carl Sagan, even admitted humbly that they would not consider themselves atheists, as though it were probable, and they have no actual *proof* to disbelieve. Dawkins corrected this when he said that as scientists, we should assume that out of *probability* in lieu of all facts, as I have stated previously as well, God does not exist. Regardless of where they stand philosophically, whether or not they are on the verge of hopping off the rails into full blown disbelief, in the long-run it won't make a difference. Read the words of the Bible or Qua'ran, they will be joining me, Hitchens, Dawkins, Russell, Buffet, Gates, Muslims if you are Christian, Christians if you are Muslim, Catholics if you are Protestant, Protestant if you are Catholics, homosexuals, aborigines, unscathed island dwellers, and your neighbor Tim who one time complimented your lawn, in a massive, intellectual, scientific, flamboyant, Hawaii modeled Hell-fest just for *questioning* the idea of God. I suppose it's time to draw your lines; if we are wrong, it is going to be much more entertaining to spend eternity in Hell with the rest of us than say, the Falwell's in Heaven.

When I was a kid one of my favorite past-times was to go to the fair whenever the season came about. As a child, the simplest things enamor you; for me, it was the "Ring Toss." "Shooting Gallery," and more importantly, "Whack-A-Mole." I will describe the latter for either the sake of nostalgia, or for some, ignorance. This game consisted of one "mole" (could be a fish, dog, gorilla, etc.) which popped up from a series of nine or so holes, and me with a hammer. The purpose of the game: bash that mole on its cranium as many times as possible to keep it from surfacing. I look at this book as a massive hammer, and the religious, as moles that keep on trying to breathe at the surface. It is for the average person to grasp hold of, shake upside down like a kid with covetable lunch money, and use to their advantage. I have been debating with religious people for quite some time now, and they will *always* poke their heads up in times of great inconvenience. If you wait long enough, and maintain an air of certainty and conviction, however, they will inevitably fall; you may walk away with that life-size King Kong doll after all.

We can continue to discredit the *people* behind the ideologies, but have consistently failed to do anything to the ideologies themselves. Ideas are powerful, and if used appropriately, can promote great things. Unfortunately, this has not always been the case. There have already been generations of individuals oppressed for a myriad of reasons, and nothing remains by which they can be truly rectified. The only thing we can do today is insure that these things do not persist into future generations. Until then, we will have the candid individuals who will shout things about evolution, carbon dating, abortion, stem cell research, and the like without much scientific backbone. This is actually a promising thing; it shows that the religious authorities who so feverishly pursued these intellectual avenues are now drowning in their own words.

As any lifeguard knows (or person who may or may not have seen *Baywatch* in its heyday), if you are not prepared to save an individual who is drowning, they will go about drowning you as well. As their struggles persevere, the thrashing, gnawing, and gnashing will actually bring you down with them. It is up to the lifeguard to promote their safety, and at times, there is only so far they can go to save that drowning person. This is unfortunately the position those who come to the door in the early hours of the morning preaching to your children, and dedicating their short life-spans to God find themselves in. They, like Mother Theresa, are consciously aware that God is not answering their prayers. They know that the opposite of love is not hate, but indifference, and that causes them to question their faith on a daily basis. Of course, every now and then there is a "miraculous" incident by which they avoided a car accident, or maybe avoided burning their toast at the last moment, at which point they casually "thank God" and move along with their day. They must live with the fact that their God is simply *indifferent* to their suffering, happiness, and subsequent indifferences to those around them; like the kid who got bored with the magnifying glass and stepped on the anthill instead.

It is time, now more than ever, to eliminate the God factor from worldly decision making. The Falwells, Christs, Muhammeds, Hitlers, and Pots provided us with frighteningly powerful speeches and philosophies. They developed beyond their own walls into terrible genocides, persecutions, and social injustices against humanities. It has given people who hear voices in their head a forum in which they can voice opinions that, although ridiculous, persuade the innocent individuals looking for answers. Like smoking, perhaps we need to pass a law that places labels on churches, stating: "May be harmful for one's health" on their walls. The people who have claimed to see the ghosts of Christmas Past need to be clinically analyzed and severely limited as we would do someone who was, by *definition*, unfit to operate machinery, drive a car, or walk through public parks.

Nelson Mandela in prison memorized (and repeated to himself daily) the poem "Invictus" because he knew that what others were saying was not true, even though they were using scripture to justify it. Learn everything you can about this man, because just as we know there are no gods, no savior Jesus Christ, no prophets like Joseph Smith and Mohammed, Mandela changed the world. He fought hate without a religious agenda, fought intolerance, stood up to authority, and defined what it meant to be a master of free-will with the following verses from "Invictus":

I am the master of my fate:

I am the captain of my soul.

In light of all his achievements, Mandela has had many monuments, writings, and statues dedicated to him. But statues have never been erected to honor the individual who said "I did it because he said so." They have been raised for those who questioned the authoritarian, unjust, and inappropriate social views of their culture in their given period in history. You have just one life; live in it, make your mark on it, and be remembered because you changed it, rather than watch it pass you by indifferently.   You can stimulate and uphold your own system of what is "right" and "wrong" today, and it is through this that religious authority will be greatly diminished.

I will never understand the instance where one is a "born-again Christian." I think this is logically inert. When one is born, there is absolutely *zero* perception of the supernatural, or for that matter a care in the world for one's actual origins. There are no cognitive belief systems, Heavens or Hells, religiously political inclinations, or care about tomorrow. You are essentially born without belief. You are born an atheist. It is only through the manipulations of your parents and religious authorities (in all realms of society) that promote religiosity. There can be no argument for "nature" over "nurture" in terms of one's spirituality. It is not inherent biologically to a species. It is only by being a "born-again atheist" that one can truly become free of all of God's hypocrisies and terrorizing; even the Orwellian thought crimes posed by the Ten Commandments. As a born-again atheist, you will do things not because you fear punishment for not doing them, but because you want to promote the goodness of the world for the sake of your children, grandchildren, and subsequent generations that follow them. That is a world in which we should live in, and a world I will dedicate my life to promoting.

# Quick Religious References for the Atheist

**Qu'ran**

**9:29** Fight those who believe not in Allah nor the Last Day, nor hold that forbidden which hath been forbidden by Allah and His Messenger, nor acknowledge the religion of Truth, (even if they are) of the People of the Book, until they pay the Jizya with willing submission, and feel themselves subdued. (Jizya is the money that non-Muslims must pay to their Muslim overlords in a pure Islamic state.)

**22:38** Surely Allah does not love any one who is unfaithful, ungrateful.

**3:32** Obey Allah and His Messenger": But if they turn back, Allah loveth not those who reject Faith.

**4:56** Those who reject our Signs, We shall soon cast into the Fire: as often as their skins are roasted through, We shall change them for fresh skins, that they may taste the penalty: for Allah is Exalted in Power, Wise.

**3:10** (As for) those who disbelieve, surely neither their wealth nor their children shall avail them in the least against Allah, and these it is who are the fuel of the fire.

**5:51** O ye who believe! Take not the Jews and the Christians for friends. They are friends one to another. He among you who taketh them for friends is (one) of them. Lo! Allah guideth not wrongdoing folk.

**5:17- 5:73-** Christians are blasphemers who have invented a lie about Allah (**10:68-69**) by ascribing partners to Allah (ie. Jesus and the Holly Ghost). Inventing a lie about Allah is the worst of sins (**7:37, 29:68**) and for this reason Christians are condemned to Hell (**10:70**).

**Volume 9, Book 84, Number 57:**

Narrated 'Ikrima: Some Zanadiqa (atheists) were brought to 'Ali and he burnt them. The news of this event, reached Ibn 'Abbas who said, "If I had been in his place, I would not have burnt them, as Allah's Apostle forbade it, saying, 'Do not punish anybody with Allah's punishment (fire).' I would have killed them according to the statement of Allah's Apostle, 'Whoever changed his Islamic religion, then kill him.'"

**8:39** And fight them until there is no more ftna (unbelief, worshipping others beside Allah), and religion is all for Allah…

**13:41** See they not that We gradually reduce the land (in their control) from its outlying borders? (See also 21:44)

**68:44** We shall punish them gradually from directions they perceive not.

**33:27** And He made you heirs to their land and their dwellings and their property, and (to) a land which you have not yet trodden, and Allah has power over all things.

**8:65** O Prophet! Exhort the believers to fight. If there be of you twenty steadfast they shall overcome two hundred, and if there be of you a hundred (steadfast) they shall overcome a thousand of those who disbelieve, because they (the disbelievers) are a folk without intelligence

**4:34** Men are in charge of women by [right of] what Allah has given one over the other and what they spend [for maintenance] from their wealth. So righteous women are devoutly obedient, guarding in [the husband's] absence what Allah would have them guard. But those [wives] from whom you fear arrogance - [first] advise them; [then if they persist], forsake them in bed; and [finally], strike them. But if they obey you [once more], seek no means against them. Indeed, Allah is ever Exalted and Grand.

**9:5** Fight and kill the disbelievers wherever you find them, take the captive, harass them, lie in wait and ambush them using every stratagem of war.

**8:39** Fight them until all opposition ends and all submit to Allah.

## Bible

**Revelation 14:4** These are they which were not defiled with women
**I Timothy 2:11-14** A woman should learn in quietness and full submission. I don't permit a woman to teach or to have authority over a man; she must be silent. For Adam was formed first, then Eve. And Adam was not the one deceived; it was the woman who was deceived and became a sinner"
**I Corinthians 14:34-35** As in all the congregations of the saints, women should remain silent in the churches. They are not allowed to

speak, but must be in submission as the law says. If they want to inquire about something, they should ask their own husbands at home; for it is disgraceful for a woman to speak in the church.

**Deut 22:13-21** If a man takes a wife and, after lying with her, dislikes her saying, 'I married this woman, but when I approached her, I did not find proof of her virginity,' ...and no proof of the girl's virginity can be found, she shall be brought to the door of her father's house and there the men of the town shall stone her to death. She has done a disgraceful thing in Israel by being promiscuous while still in her father's house. You must purge the evil from among you.

**I Corinthians 11:3-10** Now I want you to realize that the head of every man is Christ, and the head of the woman is man, and the head of Christ is God...A man ought not to cover his head, since he is the image and glory of God; but the woman is the glory of man. For man did not come from woman, but woman from man; neither was man created for woman, but woman for man. For this reason, and because of the angels, the woman ought to have a sign of authority on her head.

**Luke 12:51-3** Suppose ye that I am come to give peace on earth? I tell you, Nay; but rather division: For from henceforth there shall be five in one house divided, three against two, and two against three. The father shall be divided against the son, and the son against the father; the mother against the daughter, and the daughter against the mother; the mother in law against her daughter in law, and the daughter in law against her mother in law.

**Mark 4:11-12** And he said unto them, Unto you it is given to know the mystery of the kingdom of God: but unto them that are without, all these things are done in parables: That seeing they may see, and not perceive; and hearing they may hear, and not understand; lest at any time they should be converted, and their sins should be forgiven them.

**Luke 14:26** If any man come to me, and hate not his father, and mother, and wife, and children,and brethren, and sisters, yea, and his own life also, he cannot be my disciple.

**Leviticus 24:16** And he that blasphemeth the name of the LORD, he shall surely be put to death, and all the congregation shall certainly stone him: as well the stranger, as he that is born in the land, when he blasphemeth the name of the LORD, shall be put to death.

**2 Kings 6:28-29** And the king said unto her, What aileth thee? And she answered, This woman said unto me, Give thy son, that we may eat him to day, and we will eat my son tomorrow. So we boiled my son, and did eat him: and I said unto her on the next day, Give thy son, that we may eat him: and she hath hid her son

# INDEX

Made in the USA
Lexington, KY
17 October 2016